GW00340749

J. Whitaker
40 Gillitt Road
Hillcrest 3610
South Africa
Tel 751979

Don Hinson
The Author

Don Hinson has been a keen walker for many years and has also written 'Discovering Walks in Lakeland Mountains', 'Walks in the Snowdonia Mountains' and 'Walks in North Snowdonia'. Before retiring he taught Physics and compiled books of Physics Exercises.

ISBN 0946328 27 7

CHILTERN HILL WALKS
Don Hinson

Thornhill Press
24 Moorend Road
Cheltenham
Glos
MCMXC

ISBN 0946328 27 7
© Don Hinson, 1990

Typset by
CTL

Printed in Great Britain by
Billing & Sons Ltd, Worcester

CONTENTS

Upland fields near Cadmore End (Walk 6, stage 28)

LIST OF WALKS

MAP OF WALKS (paths are sufficiently accurate to show which maps are needed. Detailed maps accompany the text of each walk).

Dashed lines show the main walks.
Solid lines show where two walks use the same path.
Dotted lines show additional paths used in the shorter walks.
Straight lines show the edge of the 1:25000 (2½") maps.
Double straight lines show the edges of the 1:50000 (1¼") maps needed — numbers 165, 166, 175.

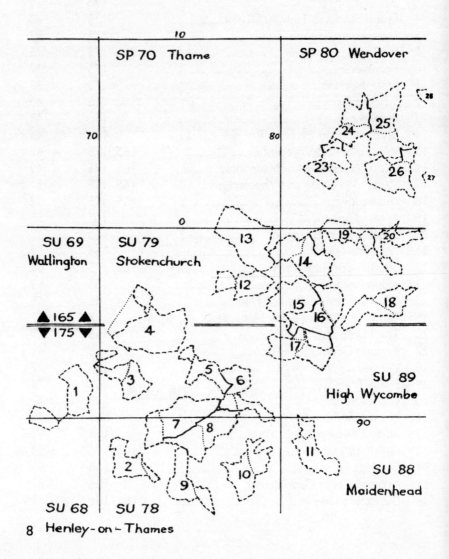

Henley-on-Thames

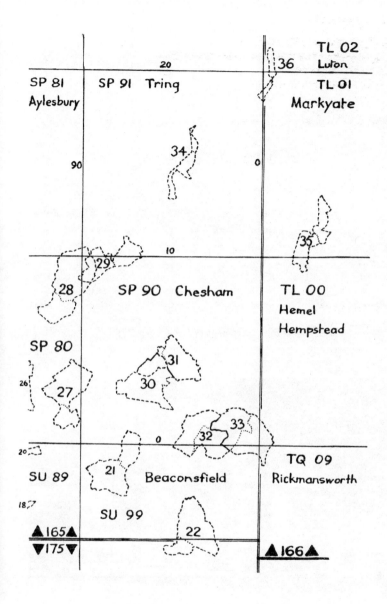

SP 81
Aylesbury

SP 91   Tring

20

TL 02
Luton

36

TL 01
Markyate

90

34

0

10

29

35

28

SP 90   Chesham

TL 00
Hemel
Hempstead

SP 80

31

30

26

27

32   33

0

20

21

SU 89

Beaconsfield

TQ 09
Rickmansworth

18

SU 99

▲165▲
▼175▼

22

▲166▲

Descending the escarpment (Walk 4, stage 23)

Turville Hill (Walk 5)

INTRODUCTION

This book describes 35 **circular** walks of about 12km (7½ miles) and 46 of about 8km (5 miles) in the Chiltern Hills, an area of outstanding natural beauty. Some of its special points are listed here:

- Routes selected to reveal the natural beauty of the countryside, with particular emphasis on the views and hills.
- Comprehensive coverage of the scenic areas.
- Written description of route always beside the relevant map — not on another page.
- Route numbers on map and written description make it easy to relate one to the other.
- Large scale maps: 2 inches per mile or 32 mm per kilometre.
- Checklist of items to take on your walk.

THE CHILTERNS

The Saxon word 'chilt' means chalk, and it is the chalk that helps to make the Chilterns an outstandingly beautiful area. There is something for everyone to enjoy: the wonderful views from the chalk downs or the carpet of flowers on them, from fragrant thyme to exotic orchids; the glorious beech woods — majestic without leaves in winter, brilliant green when fresh in spring, or best of all in autumn tints which must be seen to be believed; the unspoilt rural villages, many with Churches of special interest; the pattern of fields reflecting the dominance of agriculture, with little industrialisation.

When you add to all this a network of 2400km (1500 miles) of public paths, you have a wonderful opportunity of exploring this beautiful countryside on foot.

If you want a detailed background to the Chilterns, try Brian J. Bailey's 'View of the Chilterns' (published by Robert Hale, 1979). It is very readable, thanks to the author's sense of humour and refreshing outlook. (If you enjoy pining over the past and moaning about anything that changes, don't read it).

HOW TO FOLLOW A ROUTE

As well as this book, it is highly desirable to bring a 1:50000 (1¼ inch to the mile) map along with you. (A 1:25000 map is a luxury you don't really need — I never used one until I began writing this book). It is useful to mark the route on the map in pencil.

To fit on one page, the written descriptions of the route are brief, but, I hope clear. Before using the book, browse through the glossary to get a general idea of the terms used. Note that 'up' and 'down' always refer to gradients. (Unlike everyday speech where you may go 'down' a perfectly level road to post a letter — or for that matter 'up' a level road).

Any walk can be started at any convenient point along the route. A grid reference is given for the suggested start. The first 3 numbers refer to the grid lines that indicate how far East the point is; the last 3 numbers refer to how far North. Thus, in walk number 1, 683 means the start is three tenths of the way between the vertical lines marked 68 and 69, and 903 means it is three tenths of the way between the horizontal lines marked 90 and 91.

In emergencies such as deteriorating weather or shortage of time, it may be possible to make a short cut by roads, and these are shown in the maps of this book.

ALLOWING ENOUGH TIME

It is best to find your own walking speed, but as a rough guide allow 30 minutes per mile or 20 minutes per kilometre. You will find it varies with the weather, the nature of the paths and the number of interesting distractions you meet. Make sure the walk will be over by the following times:

Oct 10 6.20pm; 20 6pm (5pm if clocks changed); 30 4.40pm;
Nov 10 4.20pm; 20 4.10pm; 30 4pm; all Dec 4pm;
Jan 10 4.20pm; 20 4.40pm; 30 5pm;
Feb 10 5.20pm; 20 5.40pm; 30 6pm;
Mar 10 6.20pm; 20 6.40pm.

TRANSPORT

The maps show the letter 'P' where cars can be parked off the road, or in a quiet side road, without causing an obstruction or annoying the cops. Parking is free unless otherwise stated. See p15 for information on buses and trains.

GLOSSARY

Please read this and the abbreviations list carefully. The words have been chosen to keep the description of the walk concise.

down	the path descends
drive	track leading to private house or farm
farmgate	gate wide enough for vehicles to get through
lane	small surfaced public road
on	keep walking in about the same direction
path	a way too narrow for vehicles
pole	conspicuous wooden device for carrying telegraph or electricity cables (or anything else the owner feels like fixing on it)
stile	device for allowing humans to climb over or through a hedge or fence, while stopping animals. The usual step or steps may or may not be present
thicket	mini-wood consisting of shrubs and/or small trees
track	a way wide enough for vehicles (could be grassy, stony, concrete or even muddy)
up	the path rises

ABBREVIATIONS

●	is a reminder that a shorter walk follows a different route at this point
cpm	contours per mile (see p14)
E	east
km	kilometre
L	turn left through about 90°. Note however that 'fork L' means take the left hand of two paths at a fork. This will not involve turning through 90° — sometimes you may not turn at all (see figures)
½ L	turn left through about 45° (see figure)
⅓ L	turn left through about 30° (see figure)
⅔ L	turn left through about 60° (see figure)

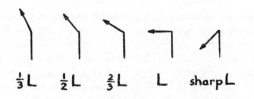 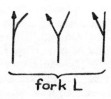

m	metre. This is roughly a yard. All distances mentioned are approximate, but near enough for purposes of following the route
mi	mile
N	north
P	parking
R	turn right through about 90°
½ R etc.	as for ½ L etc, but turn the other way
S	south
W	west
yr	your

HAZARDS AND PROBLEMS

(1) Obstructions to a public path. Happily these are rare. Sometimes a path may become overgrown or ploughed up or there may be muddy patches. You are entitled to remove an obstruction enough for you to get by, or to get round it by a short detour. If crops cover a right-of-way, you may walk through them (with care you won't do much damage anyway).

(2) Bulls. These are rare too, thank goodness. If you see a bull (binoculars can be handy here) make a wide detour and be sure you can get over the fence or gate before the bull arrives.

(3) Crossing main roads. Probably more hazardous than meeting bulls.

MAPS

The old 1" O.S. map No. 159 covered almost the whole area.

The excellent 1:50000 (1¼ ") O.S. maps No. 165 (Aylesbury & Leighton Buzzard) and 175 (Reading & Windsor) cover the area, except for walks 33 (part), 35 and 36A (most) on No. 166 (Luton & Hereford). See pp 7 — 9.

The 1:25000 (2½ ") O.S. maps (optional) for a given walk can be found from maps on pp 8 and 9.

The maps in this book are based on the ordnance survey 1:25000 1st series (or 2nd series if available) with the sanction of the Controller of Her Majesty's Stationery Office. Crown copyright reserved.

To the best of my knowledge, all paths used are public ones. Most Chiltern paths are in a reasonable condition; some are marked by white or yellow arrows. Although definitive maps showing public paths are available, there are a few anomalies e.g. in one place the owner has agreed to a rerouting of the path, and the old path is now obstructed, yet the old path remains on the map because he is unwilling to pay the administration charges required to make the change. Elsewhere I was advised not to complain about an overgrown path, because the unofficial alternative was more scenic. I am grateful for the willing help received from several County Council Offices in response to my queries about paths. Thanks also to D. Piper for telling me of a diversion in walk 35.

I hope my maps are reasonably accurate, but extra paths and features not on O.S. maps may only be shown approximately. The woods were added at a late stage, to give a general impression of how much of the route is wooded. They were based on O.S maps, so there could have been one or two changes, although important differences would have been noted while I surveyed the route.

HOW THE ROUTES WERE CHOSEN

Having spent over 150 days walking in the Chilterns and having compiled a list of about 80 different walks of around 12 km length for personal use, it occurred to me that it would be a good idea to produce a comprehensive book of Chiltern walks. While all these walks were good, some were better than others. It seemed to me that the things that make a really good walk are the views and the ever changing scene as you ramble up and down the hills. (If you are an addict of the larger hills of Britain, such as those of the Lake District, this sort of walk is about as near as you can get to these delights down South). One rough way of measuring this 'viewfulness' was to work out how many 50 foot contours the walk crossed per mile of the route. This varied from about 2 to 7 contours per mile (cpm), but in selecting the better walks I decided to omit walks with less than 4cpm.

Other important factors in choosing a route were avoiding (1) bridleways where possible, since these tend to become very muddy at times, (2) paths that were difficult to follow e.g. a confusing network of paths sometimes found in a wood, (3) roads, except where needed to link up two paths, (4) paths which do not offer much variety e.g. one entirely inside a wood or without a view for a long time.

The first edition involved a further 59 days of walking the Chiltern paths. Since then almost all the routes have been checked for this second edition. There has been little change to the routes, but addition or removal of stiles, gates, fences, etc, has required many changes to the text. Doreen, my wife, has also enjoyed these walks. Apart from doing all the typing, her comments, appreciative or critical, have helped to decide which are the best routes to use in the book.

WILD FLOWERS

The flowers of the open well drained chalky slopes are particularly attractive. Look for, but do not pick the lovely purple bellflowers, gentians and violets, the yellow rockroses, and of course, the orchids, which if you look at them closely, are every bit as beautiful as their larger exotic counterparts from the tropics. Spotted, fragrant and pyramidal orchids can be found on many of the walks described, the bee orchid on a few, and some others here and there. The best place is Bix Bottom (see summary of walk no. 2). These are ideal picnic spots, but when you sit down beware of the stemless thistles, and need I add, be sure to take any rubbish home.

FOOD FOR FREE

Blackberries are the only reliable harvest (mainly in September and October). Try a bramble crumble. You are bound to come across edible fungi now and again e.g. shaggy ink caps, blewits, puffballs, parasol, oyster, horse and field mushrooms. Don't eat them unless you are certain they are edible. There is even a mildly poisonous one just like the mushrooms sold in shops. It can be identified by the fact that the base of the stem goes yellow when cut. But if you find a white spherical fungus over 5" across with no stem, which is pure white inside, it must be the giant puffball. It is delicious cut in slices and fried in butter for 5 to 10 minutes. Try a small piece first, as (like many other foods) a few people may be upset by it.

BUILDINGS

The walks were not designed to pass by stately homes, Churches or villages. Even so, many of them can be seen on or close to the chosen routes, so brief details are given in the summaries.

BUSES

These run near most of the walks in the book, though in some cases the services are limited and may be less frequent (or even absent) at weekends. It is best to make enquiries before setting out.

TRAINS (all frequent)

Euston-Tring (34). Also to (29) via bus.
Baker St.-Amersham-G. Missenden (27)-Wendover (25).
Paddington-Henley, then buses.
Marylebone-High Wycombe, then buses.

MAP SYMBOLS

Main walk ⌇⌇⌇⌇⌇   Building ●   Bridge ⪥

Path used only in
    shorter walk ‑‑‑‑‑‑   Wood ⌓   Pond o

                                          Bus stop ⥿

Alternative path ·.
    described   Tree or pole ·
    in summary ·····   Hedge ‑‑‑‑‑   km grid lines

Road ≈ = ⁼ ⁼   Fence ⁺⁺⁺⁺⁺   ⁹ᐟ

Railway ▬▬▬▬▬▬   Wall ‑‑‑‑ᴶ   ₀₅ ─┼─

SCALE OF MAPS : 2 inches = 1 MILE; 32mm = 1 km

THE WALKS

(a ● in the text indicates the point
where the shorter walk may be taken)

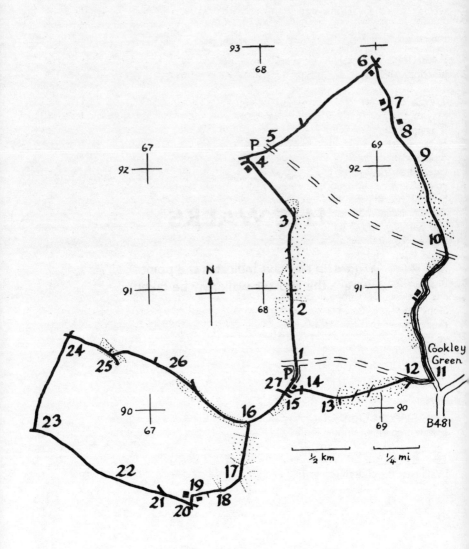

93 68

6 ✗

7

8

P 5

4

9

67
92

69
92

3

10

N

91

91

68

2

Cookley
Green

24

25 26

1

27 P

14

11

12

23

90
67

16

15

13

90
69

B481

22

17

21

19

20 18

½ km

¼ mi

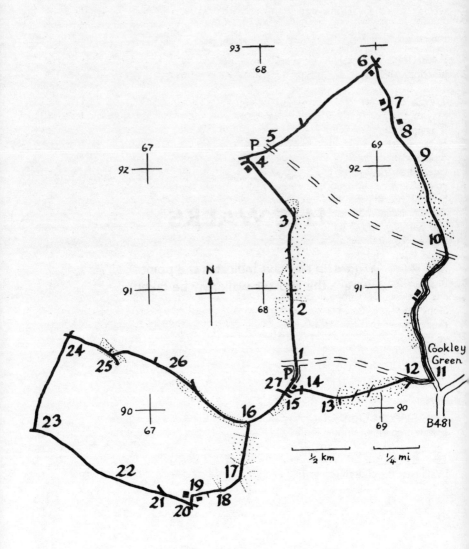

18

1 EWELME AND SWYNCOMBE DOWNS (14km, 8¾ mi, 4.8 cpm)

The downs make easy walking with wide views. There are also attractive beech woods to enjoy. There is a manor house and a small church (partly 11th century) at Swyncombe. A 14th century bell is among items of interest inside the church.

PARKING At Cookley Green turn W off the B481 and at once go L at a junction. After 1 km (¾ mi) turn L and park near the church (683 903).

1 Walk back (N) to the road turning and go on down track. 2 On into wood. Stay on the main path. 3 Track bears L to farm. 4 Just after farm, go R 40m then R again. 5 On over road. 6 At junction of 5 tracks near house, go sharp R along surfaced drive. 7 On between hedges where drive turns R. 8 After houses, go on along shady track. 9 On through wood to road. 10 Over road and ½ R along lane. 11 Sharp R along road. 12 Ignore track at wood edge, but 50m further on, go ½ L over stile. Ignore crossing tracks. 13 Go ⅓ R over field to small iron gate 30 m L of pole. 14 On over drive; R into churchyard. Pass L of church. 15 Turn L down wide bridleway. 16 At signpost, go L up field to wood. On into, and out of wood. 17 On along field edge. Bear ½ R along edge to stile in field corner. 18 Here on along track. 19 Pass barn on yr L, then turn L for 100m to cross-track. 20 Here R down track. 21 Where stony track ends keep on along L edge of field. (Ignore track along R edge.) 22 On in next fields with fence on yr R. 23 300m after fence ends turn R along track. 24 Turn R along drive beside line of trees. 25 Ignore first path on L, but 50 m before drive bears R go ½ L along small bridleway in wood. At gap leave wood and go on along field edge (hedge on yr L). Soon bear R with hedge. 26 On in wood. 27 Pass Church (on yr R).

1A SWYNCOMBE DOWNS (8 km, 5 mi, 4.6 cpm)
Follow 1 to 14, then turn R along lane past church.

1B EWELME DOWNS (6 km, 3¾ mi, 5.1 cpm)
Walk past the church (on yr L) and on down wide bridleway. Follow 16 to 27.

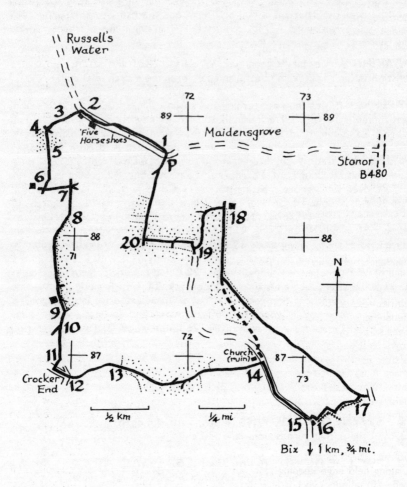

Russell's
Water

72   73
89 +   + 89

3 2
4
'Five
Horseshoes'   Maidensgrove

1
P   Stonor
B480

18

20   88
8   +   +
88
71   19

N
↑

9

10
72
+   Church
(ruin)   87
11   87   +
+   73
Crocker
12   13   14
End

½ km   ¼ mi   15   16   17

Bix ↓ 1 km, ¾ mi.

2 AROUND BIX BOTTOM (10½ km, 6½ mi, 5.7 cpm)

After leaving the road there are lovely views as you walk on either side of Bix Bottom, then a brief flatter section near Crocker End before you descend a fine beech wood and further explore the Bottom, passing the ruins of St James' Church. The ridge climb (17-18) is shady, but there are many places where views may be enjoyed, especially in winter. Finally more woodland, with the added interest of the nature reserve.

The Warburg Nature Reserve is the most interesting one in the Chilterns, consisting of 247 acres of chalk woodland, scrub and grassland. The woodland slopes are typically beech covered, and the open places support a rich variety of chalk-loving plants. Special mention must be made of the orchids, of which 17 species grow here, some in the woods, others in the open. In summer many different kinds of butterflies add a further splash of colour to the flowers.

There is an information centre at 720 880. Unlike most BBONT reserves, this one is open to the public but you are asked to stay on the public footpaths and keep dogs on leads. Further information can be obtained from BBONT (Berkshire, Buckinghamshire & Oxfordshire Naturalists' Trust), 122, Church Way, Iffley, Oxford, OX4 4EG.

PARKING. Park near the right angle bend (717 887) ½ km (¼ mi) W of Maidensgrove. (This minor road joins the B480 at Stonor.)

1 Walk NW away from Maidensgrove beside road. 2 100m past The Five Horseshoes & 20 m past house on L, turn L through gate. Go down 2 fields (fence on yr R). 3 On into 3rd field and ⅓ R down to bottom corner. 4 On over stile & on 10m over next stile, then ½ L gently up in trees. 5 On over field towards R end of distant line of trees. Later make for stile 100m L of farm. 6 ½ R over field to next stile, then L along track. 7 Where track comes in on L, go sharp R up field to far corner. 8 Here, ½ R up by wood edge (fence on yr L) until 100m past farm. 9 Then, ½ R along drive 100m. 10 At stile, go on over field, passing just R of first clump of trees, to stile. 11 On to road and L. 12 Where road turns R, keep on 100m to stile, and on along field edge (hedge on yr R). 13 On into wood. Ignore track forking L not long before leaving wood. On down fields. ● 14 Go R along road, passing farm on R, to gate just before houses. 15 Here go L and soon R along bottom edge of field to gate. Here turn L along field edge keeping fence or hedge on yr R. 16 At fence junction (with wide gap in fence) go L, still with fence on yr R. 17 Over bottom stile and sharp L up shady path. 18 Just before farm at top, go sharp L through gap into reserve. Ignore paths going off R. 19 At bottom, turn R along track and go through car park. Then turn L along an open strip of grassland. 20 At end of strip go on 20m and R up track.

2A SHORTER WALK (8½ km, 5¼ mi, 5.9cpm)

Follow 1-13, then L along road 150m, and R up track into wood. Now follow 18-21.

21

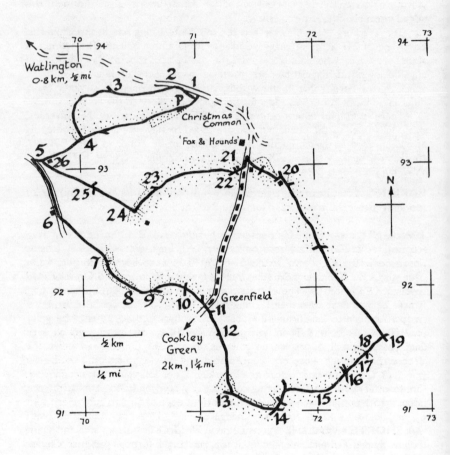

Watlington
0.8 km, ½ mi

Christmas Common

'Fox & Hounds'

Greenfield

Cookley
Green
2 km, 1¼ mi

N

½ km

¼ mi

3 WATLINGTON (11½ km, 7¼ mi, 5.7cpm)

The walk starts with a splendid introduction to the chalky Watlington Hill, then runs through fields and woods to Greenfield. Soon there is a long wooded section, but with variety in the trees and paths used. (From 16 to 17 may be a little overgrown.) More views as you reach Hollandridge and before you pass through the next stretch of woodland. The final section gives a fine view of Watlington Hill before climbing along its S side among chalkland flowers.

PARK in Watlington Hill car park (710 936) 2km (1¼ mi) SE of Watlington.

1 Go W towards Watlington beside road for 200m to gate. 2 Go ½ L through gate and along hill a little below the ridge-top, soon joining clear wide path. 3 When this has gone down for about 50m and has passed dense shrubs on yr L, fork L **down** small grass path heading towards cooling towers. It soon bears L, then goes down to pass just R of yew wood. After levelling, it enters yew wood. 4 After steps go R down path. 5 At buildings ½ R along track, then L along road. 6 50m after house go ½ L along field edge (fence on yr R). 7 On into wood. Follow path near its R edge. 8 Come out of wood to bottom of rough area, then go ½ L along path into wood. 9 After 40m fork ½ L up path. Ignore minor side turnings. 10 On over cross track. ● 11 On over road, along drive past silo on yr R. (Ignore L turn to Christmas Cottage). 12 When drive turns R go on 30m, then ½ R over field to wood. 13 On down wood and ½ L along track at bottom. 14 L along crossing track. On over second crossing track, soon climbing. After 70m, when track bears slightly L, keep on up path that bears R into wood. 15 Path bears L and widens. 16 At bottom clearing go on to its far side, go L a bit & R up small hidden path at edge of clearing. 17 Keep on as path widens. 18 On out of wood up field to far R corner. 19 Turn L along ridge track. 20 Just after house turn L along track for 20m & go ½ R along path in wood. 21 Turn L along road & ½ R along drive opposite church. 22 After going on 100m (thus ignoring 2 paths going R) turn **half** R along path. Keep on when side paths are seen. Later path widens. 23 Ignore stile on R at wood edge. Bear L to stay just inside wood. 24 On over clearing (house up on yr L), into wood for 10m, and R down field past yew tree to gate. 25 On along track. 26 After house on R & 50m before road, turn sharp R along path. 27 Soon after passing steps ignore path forking R, & gently climb beside wood edge.

3A SHORTER WALK (8½ km, 5¼ mi, 5.9cpm)

Follow 1 to 10, then L along road and sharp L along drive opposite Church. Then follow 22 onwards.

4   SHIRBURN (14km, 8¾ mi, 6.2cpm)

After a fine tour of the escarpment, the route goes gently down the side of Blackmoor Wood to a pleasant valley path. A wooded ridge is climbed, then descended to a farm before returning by a climbing path with splendid views before it enters woods. Anyone with surplus energy can enjoy the escarpment views again by following the longer-than-normal route (24-31). From 27 to 28 (and from A to 28 in the short walk) you walk on the Icknield Way, one of Britain's oldest roads — perhaps 4000 years old

The bridleway (7-8) may be the one muddy section found in damp seasons.

PARK in the woodland car park (725 955) on the minor road 2½ km (1½ mi) N of Christmas Common.

1 Take path parallel to road SW, then along road by water tower and ½ R over field to far corner. **2** Over stile and down path with wood on yr L. **3** Here path

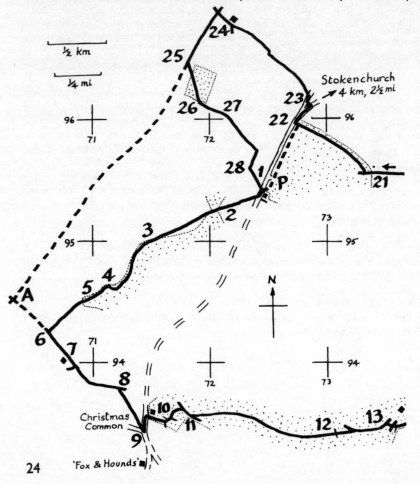

runs between wood and fence. Later it leaves fence and goes inside wood about 10m from fence. **4** After curving R, path reaches fence again, and turns L to run by it again. **5** Where fence bears R, path keeps on in thicket and past dark yews (on yr L). • **6** After descent turn L along track. **7** At buildings, on up track. **8** Near top go through gap on R at field corner, over stile and ½ R over field. On by far hedge to road. **9** L along road for 100m, then R passing just R of tower. **10** Fork ⅓ L along larger path. Soon fork L (follow arrows), then ½ R where small path comes in on L. **11** Soon path is near wood edge (on yr R). Here take L fork gently down into wood. Follow clear path first in mature, then young wood. **12** Near valley bottom go on along track that comes in on yr L. **13** 100m before buildings go R following arrows. Soon you cross a track & follow path by wood edge (on yr R). **14** R for 30m along track. ½ L up field to stile. Here on over track and down field to hedge gap. **15** Through gap and L along by hedge. **16** On along valley. Soon on along drive. **17** Ignore L fork to buildings, but 100m later go ½ L up track. After a further 100m go on up shady path when track bears R. **18** Go L down crossing path. **19** Path leaves wood & goes down field passing L of farm. Cross stile & up to next stile. **20** L along drive 60m & R up field. **21** Into wood 30m L of pole. Fork R along wood edge. • **22** Turn R along road. **23** Turn L over fence at white arrow & R along old road (parallel to present road). Soon go L down grass track. **24** On past farm, then L along track (beside poles). **25** 100m before double pole, go ½ L through gap to stile and on in wood. **26** Leave wood and go ½ L along its edge. On up to double pole. **27** ½ R along by fence (on yr L) which later turns R. **28** Go L over stile, R 5m & L up track.

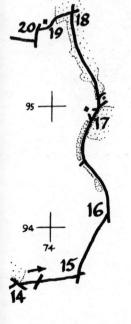

4A SLIGHTLY SHORTER WALK (11km, 7mi, 5.6cpm)

Follow 1 to 21. Then turn L along path parallel to road.

4B MUCH SHORTER WALK (6½ km, 4mi, 6.7cpm)

Follow 1 to 5. Then, after descent turn R along track. **A** R at cross track. **25** 100m past double pole go sharp R through gap to stile and on in wood. Follow 26 onwards.

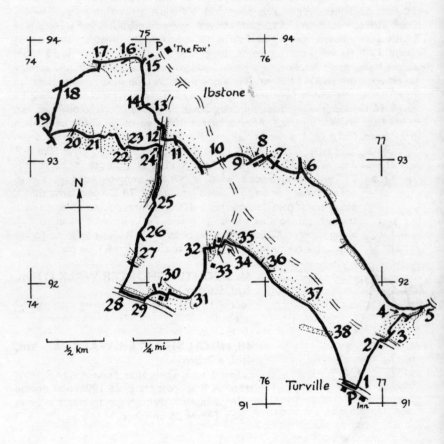

94
74

17 16 75
        P 'The Fox'
        15

94
76

18

Ibstone

19

14 13

20 21 23 12
      22 24 11

93

10   8
     9   7   6

77

93

N

25

26

27

32 35

33 34 36

37

92
74

30

28 29 31

4

5

3

2

38

92

½ km   ¼ mi

Turville
            1

76   P
            Inn

77
91

91

26

5   TURVILLE TO IBSTONE (11½ km, 7¼ mi, 7.2 cpm)

You start at Turville, a delightful village with a Medieval Church. The steep scenic start passes an old smock-mill, now converted into a house, and then drops down the other side of the ridge to a good valley path, then a wooded climb to Ibstone. There follows a switch back route of woods and views, finally a scenic gentle descent of a fine ridge.

In some seasons there will be some muddy places (e.g. at 13, 15 on the longer walk). The church at 33 is Norman.

PARK at Turville in the car park between the 'Bull and Butcher' and church (768 911).

1 Take footpath opposite phone box. Aim just L of Windmill. **2** At road go R, then L down track in wood. **3** After 100m go over stile on L and down path. **4** On entering field, turn R along edge. At corner go over stile and L down track. **5** 30m before road go sharp L along path in valley bottom. **6** Well after entering pine wood, turn L up path (by arrow on tree) which at once crosses track. **7** Cross grass track. Turn L for 20m along wide track, then go R 20m & L along field edge. **8** At field corner, ⅓ R up path for 40m. Bear R along track for 20m, and L up path to stile. **9** Here on up field, through hedge gap and up field (fence on yr R). At top go R over stile and L to road. **10** On over stile. Down ½ R in wood at second stile. **11** At bottom, cross over path & go up path by fence. ●
12 At drive turn R. Just after Ibstone Cottage go L up stony track. **13** Where it becomes grassy keep on along winding track. **14** Soon cross stony track and go ½ R along field edge (wide hedge on yr L). **15** When path bends R, go ½ L and soon L along shady track into wood. **16** On where path forks and soon descends. **17** When view is seen turn ½ L down path (No. S21) and out of wood. R along field edge to valley bottom. **18** L along track (hedge on yr R). **19** At wide stony track go L 10m and L over field to stile into wood. **20** On 10m over track, then ½ R along vague track, never far from wire fence (on yr L). **21** On over field (fence on yr L) into wood. On up path, soon winding up steep hill. **22** 20m before top edge of wood, bear L on gently climbing path. Soon R to edge of main wood. Here on through small thicket to field. **23** On over field, then between fences. On along drive to road. **24** R along road. **25** At fire hydrant near road end, go on down track just left of road. **26** Where track bends ½ L, on over stile, then down field to stile. **27** On in trees, on over track, on over field to road. **28** L down road. **29** Near white gate on L, go ½ L along track 100m to where it turns L. **30** Here go on along path that bears R to drive. Go L along drive, then R along path 30m below top edge of wood. Follow it to stile at wood edge. **31** Here, turn L up hill passing L of buildings. Keep along wood edge (on yr R) to stile by trough. **32** Go R up in wood. On over track. **33** At top where path levels, turn L, then 20m later, go R into Churchyard. Pass Church (on yr L) to lane. **34** Here turn L. On reaching road go R steeply down it. **35** Where it bends R, go on through gate on L along level track. **36** After slight descent, track bends L towards top of wood. Here go R down to fence. Keep along fence, between wood edge and fence. **37** Over stile in fence, and over second stile 10m away. Follow path down to L end of strip of trees. **38** In and out of trees by stiles, over third stile and on to houses. L to car park.

5A SHORTER WALK (9Km, 5½ mi, 6.9cpm)
Follow 1 to 11. Go L along lane, then follow 25 onwards.

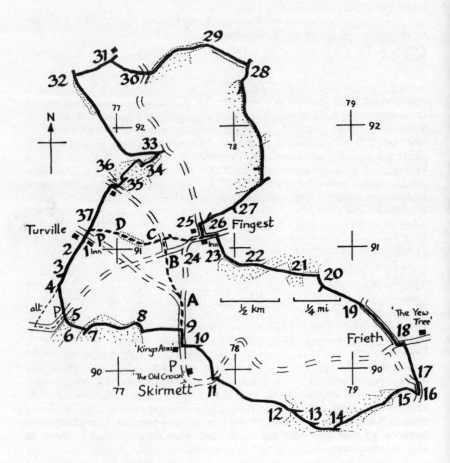

N

31
32
30
29
28
77
92
79
92
78
33
36
34
35
27
37
25 26 Fingest
Turville
D
C
91
2
Inn
B 24 23 22
21 20
3
91
4
A
alt P
½ km
¼ mi
19
'The Yew Tree'
5
8
18
6 7
9
Frieth
17
10
78
Kings Arms
16
P
90
78
90
'The Old Crown'
11
15
77
Skirmett
79
12 13 14

6   AROUND FINGEST (12½ km, 7¾ mi, 5.5 cpm)

Starting from the delightful village of Turville with its medieval Church, the walk has many fine views and passes through Skirmett, Frieth and Fingest. Fingest's Church has a Norman tower with an unusual twin-gabled roof. There are several woods which add variety without losing the views for long. The old smock-mill (now converted into a house) which is often seen during this walk, is met on the final descent.

The paths are good, but there can be a few muddy patches, e.g. 2-3, 29-30.

PARK at Turville in the car park between the 'Bull and Butcher' & church (768 911).

I Go SW up tiny road that starts by car park. 2 On up path when road ends. 3 On across field for 150m. 4 Then ½ L to gate at L corner of wood. (If there are crops and no path to gate, keep on to road just L of buildings. Here go L to reach point 5, 100m after road bends L). 5 Through gate and along track past pipeline. 6 On over field to wood. 7 Up in wood and soon L along main track. 8 Where track ends, follow path between fences R along wood edge, then L to drive and road. ● 9 R along road. L just before King's Arms. 10 Into field (pass L of house) and ½ R along field edge near line of poles (fence on yr R). 11 L at road. Soon R up track. 12 At wood, fork gently R. 13 Near top of rise fork R to wood edge. Keep on along wood edge track 100m or so. 14 Then ½ L down small path in wood. 15 Out of wood between fences to road. 16 L along road. 17 Where road bends L go on over field between fences. On to road. 18 Here L and soon R along roads. 19 Keep on when road turns R. 20 Stay on track as it turns L along wood edge. Keep on as it enters wood. 21 Track ends at wood edge. On over field into wood. 22 Out of wood and down by its edge. 23 At wood bottom ½ R (hedge on yr L) to road. L along road. ● 24 R along road. 25 R up path 50m after Church. 26 Over stile and on up fields by fence on yr R to reach track. 27 On up track. Soon fork L along wood edge. 28 After wood, follow track up. Near top go L along hedge near telegraph wires. Keep hedge on yr L in several fields. 29 After path has gone down, go ½ L into narrow wood. 30 At road, go over stile into field, keeping a level course to reach track at stile 100m L of farm. 31 ½ L along track (hedge on yr R) to bottom. 32 L along valley bottom path. 33 30m before road go sharp right up path in trees. 34 At stile, go R along field edge for 50m and L up winding path. 35 After steep climb by fence, go over large stile and up to road. 36 R for 50m, then L. Down by fence or hedge on yr L to stile. 37 On over field.

6A   SKIRMETT TO CADMORE END (9km, 5½ mi, 6cpm)
Follow 1 to 8, then L along road to fork. A On along field edge (hedge and road on yr L) to stile. On over field to 2nd stile. Here ⅓ R over field to stile. B On up road. C R along path. Soon ½ R at path junction. On along road, then L along road. Now follow 25-37.

6B   TURVILLE TO FRIETH (8km, 5mi, 4.4cpm)
Follow 1 to 23. Then 50m after Church go on along path (wall on yr L). ½ L at path junction. C On over road (soon line of beeches on yr L). D ⅓ L down field to 2nd of 2 stiles, then L to road.

7   STONOR AND THE TURVILLE DISTRICT (11½ km, 7¼ mi, 5.8cpm)

First you go through the Deer Park, passing the Elizabethan mansion (for many centuries the home of the Stonor family) and up through a wood. The ridge (5-6) beyond Southend farm is the start of a series of delightful Chiltern views. Woods are met around Maidensgrove, before the final open ridge down to Stonor.

Since overpopulation would result in starvation, a cull of the wild deer takes place in August or September and in January or February. Notices will then ask you not to use the Park path. At other times, please stay strictly on the footpath, keep **all** dogs on leads (since even well behaved ones can't always resist chasing deer) and never, never touch a fawn or it will be deserted by the doe. If the cull is in progress, go S down road 100m past T-junction and L along track that runs by wire fence (on yr L) up to road. On along road and L at junction to reach point 4.

PARK at Stonor on the B480 200m N of the T-junction, near footpath sign (737 889).

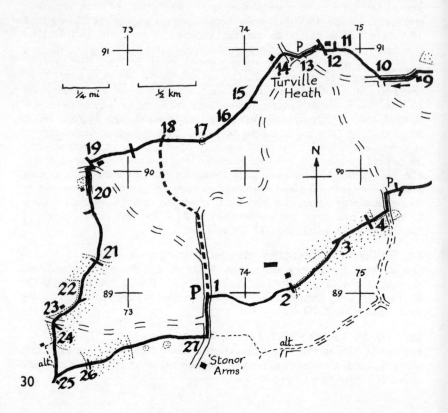

1 Follow grass path E, climbing along the valleyside. 2 After passing Stonor House, the path runs just inside thinly wooded area. Ignore crossing paths. 3 On where path joins track. 4 L along road for 150m, then R along track. 5 At farm go on down ridge (at first fence on yr R). 6 At road on over field. 7 15m before reaching hedge, turn sharp L up path past the L hand of 2 poles. 8 On up ridge, keeping wood on yr R. 9 On along road to T-junction. 10 Here ½ R over field to far hedge and on (hedge on yr R). 11 Over stile in hedge and L along hedge (on yr L). Soon on between hedges to gate. 12 Through gate and R 30m, then L along drive. 13 R along road and on along drive marked 'Saviors'. 14 On along path just L of gate. Pass house and go on over field to stile. On over stiles to gate. 15 Through gate and ½ R between fences. 16 On down fields (fence on yr R). 17 At trees bear slightly R down field to crossing track. 18 Up field (bank on yr R) over lane and down field (hedge on yr L). 19 After passing barn go L along track 50m to road. Go R along road 50m, then L along smaller road. 20 ⅓ L along track. Keep on (hedge on yr L) when track goes R. 21 On up in wood. 22 At top, keep on inside wood near its edge (on yr R) to reach road. 23 Over road and up path in wood (near edge on R). 24 At top corner, on over stile and field towards buildings. (If path is missing, retreat 20m to a gap. Cross field to a house and go L along field edge). 25 At field corner turn sharpish L over field to stile at wood edge (by tree with white mark). 26 On down wooded, then open ridge to road. 27 Here L along road past T-junction.

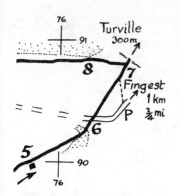

7A SHORTER WALK (9 km, 5½ mi, 4.6cpm)
Follow 1-17, then L along crossing track, R along road and on at road junction.

8   SKIRMETT TO STONOR (12km, 7½ mi, 5.9cpm)

After a scenic start, the walk passes through Stonor Deer Park (8 to 10), passing the Elizabethan mansion, which for centuries has been the home of the Stonor family. After a climb out of Stonor, there are more fine views, a flattish stretch, then some beech woods before the open descent to Skirmett.

There may be some mud in the wood (20-21).

Since overpopulation would result in starvation, a cull of the wild deer takes place in August or September and in January or February. Notices will then ask you not to use the Park path. At other times, please stay strictly on the footpath, keep **all** dogs on leads (since even well behaved ones can't always resist chasing deer) and never, never touch a fawn or it will be deserted by the doe. If the cull is in progress, use roads to reach point 12.

PARK in Skirmett near the phone box (776 901).

1 Go N along road towards Fingest. Soon go L along drive to stile. On up path.
2 R at wood between fences. **3** L up into wood at its corner. Fork R after 100m.
4 Watch for fork and go ½ R down it to wood edge, down field and on through trees to road. **5** L along road. **6** L up track near house. On past farm. ● **7** L at road. R along cross-track. **8** ½ L along path when gate seen 100m ahead down track. **9** Ignore crossing paths. Pass buildings (in valley to yr R). **10** L along road.
11 L along track, soon by wire fence on yr L. Follow fence up to road.

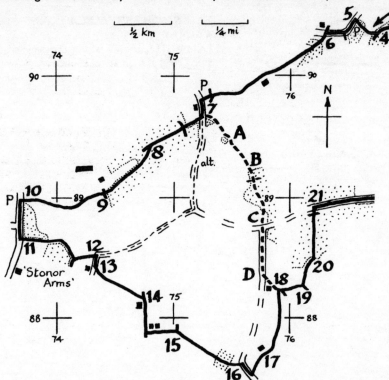

32

12 R along road 100m to stile. Here ½ L over field to stile. **13** On to stile just L of house. **14** Here R along drive and L just after farm. **15** Follow poles down field to stile. On up wood, then field, to road. **16** R up road and sharp L along drive, passing farm (on yr L). **17** On by fence (on yr R) to gate. Here go ½ L by fence (on yr L) to concrete track. ● **18** Here go R along it. Soon on along track by hedge (on yr L). **19** Go L at fork (hedge on yr L), soon beside wood. **20** At stile go L into wood. **21** R along lane. **22** After farm turn L beside fence (on yr L). At field go ½ R to wood. On down wood. At bottom go R along track 50m then L down small path out of wood. **23** Along field edge (fence on yr R) to stile, and R to road. **24** L along road. Keep on at T junction. **25** L just before road bends. Follow fence on yr L. It bears L to drive. Along drive to road and R to point 1, or L to phone box at start.

8A   WEST OF SKIRMETT (8km, 5mi, 5.4cpm)
Follow 1 to 6. Then L at road. L along cross track. Where it turns L, go on over field passing just L of clump of trees. **A** On (SE) to stile at R edge of wood. **B** On down wood. On up wood (fence on yr L). On over stile and field to road. **C** On along road. **D** ½ L along drive. **18** On over field (hedge on yr L). Now follow 19 to 25.

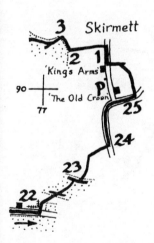

8B   AROUND STONOR (7km, 4½ mi, 5.8cpm)
PARK at Stonor on the B480 200m N of the T-junction, near footpath sign (737 889).

Go S along road past T junction. Follow 11 to 17. Then **18** L along track to road passing to R of farm. **D** ½ R along road to T junction. **C** On over field to stile. Down in wood. Up in wood to stile. **B** Go slightly L (NW) up field to clump of trees. **A** Pass just R of trees and on to gate and stile. Along track to road. On over road. Now follow 8 to 9.

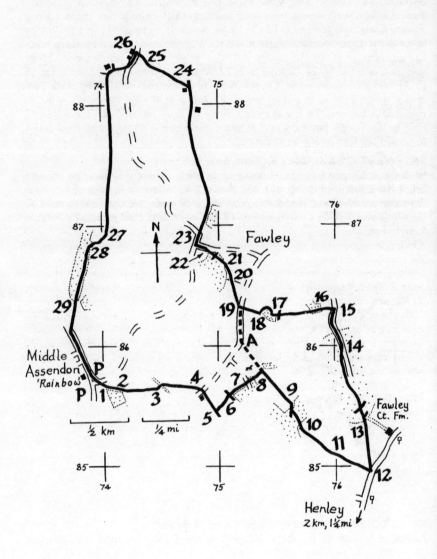

26
25
24
74
88
88
75

76
87
87

N

23
Fawley
22
21
20
27
28
19
17
16
18
15
29
A
14
86
Middle
Assendon
86
'Rainbow'
P
2
4
7
P
1
3
8
9
5
6
10
Fawley
Ct. Fm.
½ km
¼ mi
11
13
12
85
85
74
75
76

Henley
2 km, 1¼ mi

34

9   FAWLEY (11km, 6¾ mi, 6cpm)

After a steep start & fine views, some gentler gradients follow. You pass by a free mini-zoo with several unexpected animals before getting more views near Fawley Court Farm. Then a climb through a wood to open hills, the climax being the superb ridge-top walk S from Stonor.

PARK in Middle Assendon (739 857) where a minor road going E leaves the B480.

1 Go up minor road. Soon go ½ R up track. **2.** Near top of steep rise follow track ½ L. **3** Near fence go ½ L to gap in line of pines. Through gap and ½ R over field to hidden stile just L of house at L end of line of trees. **4** Over road and along track past house. **5** Look for fence coming in on yr L. Here L along fence (on yr L). **6** On over track. Along wood edge (on yr R). **7** On over road. • **8** Go R along large track. **9** At wood follow fence on yr L, thus soon leaving track. **10** On down field to gate & stile in dip. **11** Here go on to road. **12** Here turn sharp L over field. Aim for far end of line of pines. **13** Here over stile & up path in wood. Follow arrows, soon near fence on yr L. **14** On up road. **15** Turn L at footpath sign (by small red post box). Go down to L corner of wood. **16** On inside wood by its edge. On outside wood, up fields and through gates. **17** At top field corner, go through gate, over track, through gate and on along winding edge of field to stile. **18** Go over into drive and R along it. **19** Over road & ½ R to stile in fence 30m up from trees. **20** On down field edge to gate. **21** Down path in wood to road. **22** On down road. R at T-junction. **23** After 100m keep on up farm road. **24** After road levels and passes last house, ½ L over stile towards L of 2 houses. **25** At stile ⅓ R to stile just R of R hand house. **26** Here L along road 150m, R along track 150m. Bear L along ridge track. **27** When track ends, bear R by fence down to wood. **28** In wood bear L along path near its top edge. **29** On down field to road and ½ L to start.

9A   SHORTER WALK (8km, 5mi, 5.6cpm)

Follow 1 to 7, then go L along large track. **A** On along road 300m. **19** Opposite drive, go ½ L to stile in fence 30m up from trees. Now follow 20 to 29.

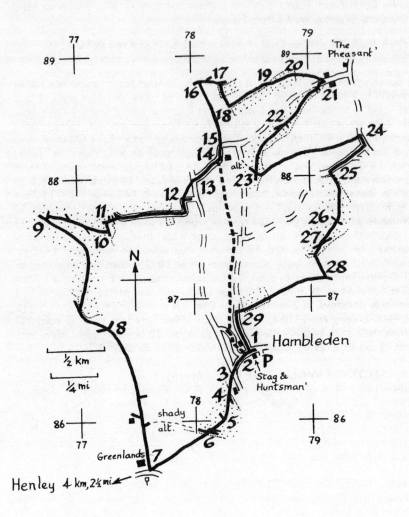

77
89

78

79
89 'The Pheasant'

17
16
19 20
21

18
22

15
14
alt.
23
24
88
25

12 13
26
27
11
9
10
28

N
87
87

29
8
1 Hambleden
2 P
3 'Stag & Huntsman'

½ km
¼ mi
4
78
shady alt.
5
86
86
77
6
79

Greenlands 7

Henley 4 km, 2½ mi

10 HAMBLEDEN (13km, 8mi, 4.7cpm)

After a good woodland climb, and fields to Greenlands Farm, you turn North up a valley, then over a wooded ridge back to the Hambleden valley. On the other side there is a fine variety of splendid views and lovely woodland, before returning to the charming old village. It has a Tudor Manor House and a 14th century Church that is full of interest e.g. the memorial to Sir Cope D'Oyley (died 1633), his wife and their numerous children (the ones holding skulls died before Mum and Dad did). There is a carved oak Gothic altar screen, said to be made from Cardinal Wolsey's bed, and a painting of the Virgin by Murillo.

PARK in Hambleden car park (785 866).

1 From the car park turn L down road. 2 When beside Church, go ½ L, soon over bridge. 3 At road junction, go on up path. 4 Take R fork up, soon after passing school. 5 When path starts to drop, ignore R turn. 6 Cross tracks at wood edge. On over field (first by fence) to road. 7 At once R along track past farm. On along valley bottom. 8 At track junction go roughly on up gently rising track. It soon bears R into wood. 9 Turn R up track that goes R after 10m. 10 When track levels at T-junction, go L. 11 At next T-junction turn R down track along wood edge. (Ignore side turnings.) Soon track is surfaced. 12 At sharp R turn go on through gate & ½ R down field to gate. 13 Go along lane opposite gate. ● 14 Soon go L with road. 15 Straight on along track where road goes R. 16 R along small road to wood. 17 Here go R up beside wood edge, over stile and on in field to wood. 18 Here L up by wood edge. 19 At stile enter wood. Keep near its edge. 20 At end of wood, go over stile and up field to buildings. Here 2 stiles lead to road. 21 Go R down road 30m & fork L into wood. Soon ignore faint & clear tracks going L & ½ L to wood edge. 22 400m later fork ⅓ L along path that gently rises at first. 23 Go L at crossing track, soon leaving wood. 24 At road go R, & soon R again. 25 At footpath sign bear L along top edge of young wood. Soon track leaves edge & turns ½ R. 26 On over cross path. 27 When parallel track is seen on yr L, move over to it. Follow it L out of wood. 28 R down track to road. 29 At road L, and L to car park (or R to 2).

10A EAST OF HAMBLEDEN (8½ km, 5¼ mi, 3.3cpm)

L out of Hambleden car park, through Churchyard, passing just L of Church. On 100m along road, then R at first signpost along clear path through fields, gardens and more fields. R at road. Now follow 14-29.

10B WEST OF HAMBLEDEN (8km, 5mi, 4cpm)

Follow 1 to 13. Just before farm, turn R along path, over fields, soon with hedge on yr R. On through gardens and fields. Finally, bear R to sign-post 100m R of Church. L along road and through Churchyard (passing R of Church).

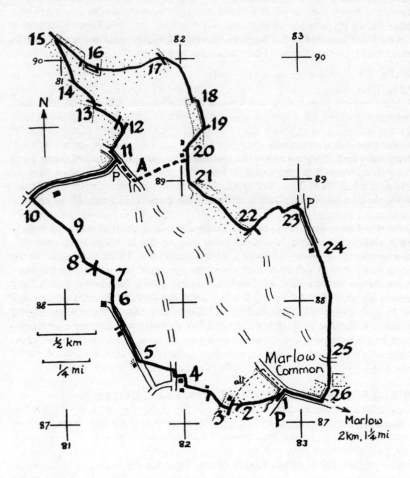

15
16
90
81
14
13
N
12
11
P
A
10
9
8
7
6
88
½ km
¼ mi
5
4
3
2
1
P
87
81
82

17
82
83
90
18
19
20
89
21
22
23
P
89
24
88
25
Marlow
Common
26
87
83
Marlow
2km, ¼ mi

38

11   NEAR MARLOW (11km, 6¾ mi, 4.6cpm)

After the wooded common there are delightful open views (right from 3-7) and an easy flatter section. There follows a long wooded interlude, relieved by 3 glimpses into the open country where the path meets the edge, and by the variety of trees encountered. After passing the attractive Bluey's Farm (19) there is a fine beech wood (21-22) and more excellent views, culminating in those from a magnificent ridge (24-25).

Paths may be muddy on the common (avoided by going NW along road at start, then L along track to point 3 after passing the last house), along stage 21 and at Copy Farm (24).

PARKING. Take the minor road from Marlow through Bovingdon Green. At T-junction turn L and park beside wooded common (829 873) 100m from junction.

1 Walk towards T-junction & go sharp L along path in wood. Keep straight on along main path. 2 When house is seen, go on along smaller path & soon go L along stony track. 3 Soon go R over stile. At wood edge go ½ R down field to stile near barn. Then ½ L up next field (hedge on yr R). 4 Over stile near houses and along path between fences. Go R along road 60m & ½ L up field to stile by house and a few pines. 5 R along road. 6 At Woodend House go on along track. On down field (hedge on yr L). 7 L over stile (hedge on yr L). Later on over track. (Here ignore stile on L.) 8 When hedge goes L you go ½ R towards buildings. 9 ⅓L over stiles (now fence on yr R). ● 10 R along road and L at T-junction. 11 At footpath sign go R up path along wood edge. 12 Bear L off bank to follow arrow. The path crosses track & widens to become a track. 13 At wood edge go ½ R with track, & cross over a track. (Your track now bears L.) 14 At end of long straight section fork ⅓R (arrow on tree). 15 At wood edge go sharp R along valley path. 16 On out of wood and soon in again. (Or follow track round edge of field.) 17 At wood edge ½ R up rough field to top fence & hedge. Walk beside them (on yr L). 18 Into wood & L up its edge to stile. Over stile & R along wood edge. 19 Over stile & down track. 20 30m before house go ½ L along path by line of pines. On over stiles. On to wood (fence on yr L). 21 L over stile & up into wood. Keep on to its far corner. 22 Here bear L up track. 23 Bear R along road. 24 On through farm, over field and down ridge. 25 On over road. 26 R along road and L at T-junction.

11A SHORTER WALK (8½ km, 5¼ mi, 5.1cpm)

Follow 1-9, then R along road and R at T junction. A At next junction sharp L along farm track. Follow path up grass. Go R at 2 stiles & on to wood (fence on yr L). Now follow 21 to 26.

12 STOKENCHURCH (11½ km, 7¼ mi, 6.9cpm)

The walk goes down fields to the beeches of Crowell Wood, over the wooded ridge and over an open ridge to Town End. Then some fine views along the foot of the Bledlow Ridge, before returning through The City, some flat fields, a splendid beech wood and up a final gentle ridge.

There may be muddy patches between 18 and 19; 7 and 8.

Radnage Church has been there for 600 years and its Norman tower was built around 1200 A.D. It has a Saxon font, fragments of medieval murals and a fine nave roof (1470 A.D.)

PARK at Stokenchurch on quiet side roads near the Green (761 963).

1 Along road shown on map behind 'Kings Arms', and along The Lane, which starts by 'Royal Oak'. **2** After Mallard's Court, at double footpath sign on R, fork L down drive with wood on yr L. **3** Soon track bears L into wood. Here over stile and down field to its opposite corner. **4** Here go down field by fence on yr L, over track & field to hidden stile in hedge. On over field to wood. **5** Follow arrows up path that starts 50m L of wood corner. **6** At top follow arrows on down path. **7** R along track at bottom near wood edge. **8** On out of wood. **9** At footpath sign go sharp L up field to hedge gap. **10** Here ½ R over stile & beside hedge (on yr R). Soon go R over stiles & drive. **11** Here ½ R towards bungalow. Go L of this along concrete path and down field (hedge on yr L). **12** Through hidden gate in field corner. On down past house (on yr R) to road. Down road 150m; L 100m along road; R over field to Church. **13** On through Church gate, (keeping near wall on yr R). Over steps in wall and ½ R down field to stile. **14** Here ½ R over field to stile at wood edge. **15** Go along by wood edge through fields. **16** At end of wood keep on by hedge. **17** When hedge bears R 250m before it reaches road, go ½ L through small gap & up between fences. **18** Over

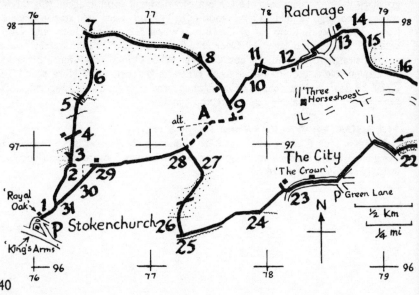

iron steps and R down track. **19** Leave track at next iron steps. On down field to road. **20** R 50m, then L across field to wood. **21** R up wood to road. **22** Go R along road. Soon L up track & R along road. **23** As road bears L, go ⅓ R along Pophley's drive 50m, then on along path. In field go ⅓ L to end of hedge. **24** Here ½ R along grass track in open field. **25** Near far end of hedge turn R over field to wood. **26** On in wood. Path bears R and drops. Ignore cross track. **27** After wood go on (NW) down field with hedge on yr R, then up. ● **28** At track turn L up ridge (fence on yr R). **29** At house go ½ L over field to pole (or on 100m & L along field edge). **30** Here go on near shallow valley bottom with fence on yr R, to reach lane. **31** Here L for Stokenchurch, or R to follow point 2 onwards.

12A   RADNAGE (7½ km, 4¾ mi, 6.7cpm)
Park in quiet side roads in The City (786 967). Walk W along road and follow 23 to 27. Then, as track starts to go down again, go R down field (if no path, go on to bottom and R). **A** At bottom, R along track, then L along track 100m. **9** ½ R up field to hedge gap. Now follow 10 to 22.

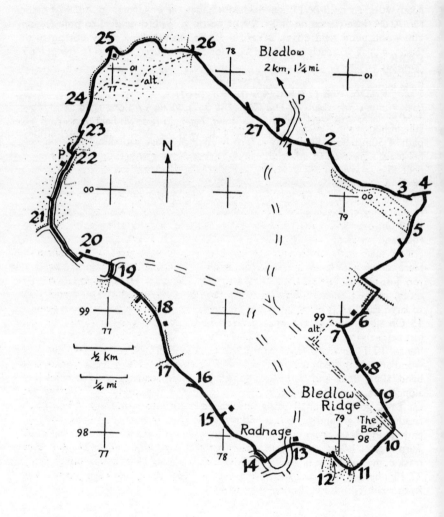

25
26
78
Bledlow
2 km, 1¼ mi
01
01
alt
24
23
27 P
P
2
22
P
N
3 4
00
00
21
79
5
20
19
18
99
77
99
alt
6
7
½ km
8
¼ mi
17
16
9
Bledlow
Ridge
15
79
'The
Boot'
10
98
Radnage
98
77
14
13
11
12

13 BLEDLOW (11km, 7mi, 5.4cpm)

The walk starts over the tiny isolated Lodge Hill with its abundance of lovely flowers. Then there is a climb up to Bledlow Ridge with wide views. More views down the other side and a gentle climb to the wooded escarpment, before returning over fields.

Mud may be found at 6 (one short bit), 7 (could avoid by going on up to road), 10-11, and 25-26 avoided by this attractive alternative:

At 24, when path starts to descend gently by wood edge, go ½ R along path into wood, soon gently climbing the ridge along wide track. Rejoin walk at 26.

PARK in layby (784 005) on the minor road 3km (1¾ mi) S of its junction with the B4009 (near Bledlow). The layby is by a footpath signpost and is 200m S of a bend in the road.

1 Over stile opposite layby and SE across 2 fields towards Lodge Hill. **2** Over stile in hedge and R along path, soon climbing hill. **3** ½ L 50m to stile and down path. **4** 50m before field corner, turn R through hedge gap along track skirting hill (rough grass on yr R). **5** On through hedge gap, down & up fields. Keep by field edge to wood corner. Here turn L by fence to gate, then R up by fence (on yr R). **6** On up lane. **7** Go L at signposted path between shrubs & fence. Soon on along lower edge of field. Follow path to gate 50m R of edge. **8** Here on over lane & along enclosed path. Soon over stile and on along field edge (hedge on yr R). **9** On over stile, now hedge on yr L. Then on along drive to road. **10** Over road and on along path. **11** Ignore path going off down on L just inside wood. Follow main path which soon curves L to reach open ground (with shrubs). Here, down path keeping near trees on yr R. **12** Soon there are trees on yr L too. Just as they end go L down path to stile. Over 2 fields towards Church (in trees) and ½ L through Churchyard to road. **13** Over road and on across field to large gate. **14** R along road and on along surfaced drive where road goes L. **15** On along track where drive goes R. **16** Where track narrows and bears L just before gate, keep on through gate over field. Make for far hedge going up to house. **17** Follow this hedge up (keep it on yr R). **18** On over stile through wood and along field edge (hedge on yr R) to road. **19** Here R along road. L at bend, along track and past buildings. **20** Just after buildings go L to road & R along it. **21** At bend go R along Hill Top Lane. **22** Just past Hill Top Cottage and car park, go L & soon R along unsurfaced track into wood. **23** When track reaches open ground go ½ L for 50m & R along fairly level grass path. **24** Soon path gently descends among trees. Later walk on L bank of sunken path. **25** Turn R after house on R. Path becomes track along wood edge. **26** 50m after track comes up on yr L, go R over stile and ½ L along field (fence 10m to yr L). **27** 10m before fence turns R, go L over stile and R along field edge (fence on yr R) to road. Turn L for 10m to reach point 1.

14 BRADENHAM TO BLEDLOW RIDGE (13km, 8mi, 5.5cpm)

After beech woods, Bradenham is approached over fields. It is a beautiful unspoilt village, with cottages, farms, manor (home of Disraeli's father) and Church (15th century tower; Norman S doorway) set around a large green. Then along a ridge (8-13), crossing briefly to Bledlow Ridge before ending on Callows Hill — yet another ridge. Only a few short wooded sections, so plenty of extensive views. The only blemish is the factory near Slough Hill.

PARKING. At Saunderton leave the A4010 and go NE 1km (½ mi) up the minor road to car park (823 990).

1 Go S along signposted track through gate and on between hedges. It climbs gently along wood edge and soon bears L up away from edge (ignore small tracks leaving main one). **2** When path levels, fork L. **3** Leave woodland paths & go ½ R along dry track curving L then R past windowless building. **4** The valley track leaves wood bearing R. **5** L at cross track to reach road by Church. **6** R down road. **7** R at main road for 50m, then ½ L through gate. Over railway and on over field to stile in hedge. **8** Slant gently up next field. Aim to reach trees

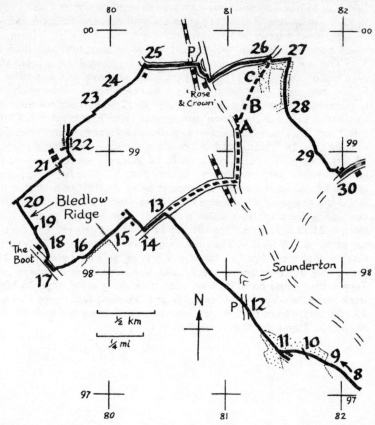

ahead about 70m L of their R hand edge. **9** Here at stile, go on into wood. **10** Soon go on over a wider path. **11** On reaching a track, bear R (keep on when second track comes in from L). **12** On over road and up hill. ● **13** L at road. **14** R at staggered cross road along track for 150m, then L over stile and field to stile at hedge corner. **15** Here on up field edge (hedge on yr L). **16** Over stile and ½ R up next field. Over stile and between fences to road. **17** R along road 100m, and R along rough road. **18** At its end, go over stile and on by hedge on yr R to reach 2nd stile. **19** Here, over stile and on along field edge (hedge on yr L). **20** Over stile and soon R down lane and field to bottom L corner stile. Here bear L to farm & R along track. **21** Turn L at track junction. **22** After 80m go on along path where track goes L to farm. Then 80m later, go ½ R along track. At hedge go L to stile & R towards pylon. **23** On to stile by pylon (hedge on yr L). **24** On by field edge (hedge on yr R). Near houses, bear L along field edge to stile at road. **25** R along road, R after bridge, R along main road and L along road until it bends L. **26** Here go R over stile & at once L over stile up field by wood edge. **27** At top, R over stile and along in wood. **28** Leave wood. Keep on along field edges (hedge on yr L), down ridge. **29** Follow track after hedge stops. At fence go R 40m to road. **30** L along road.

14A BRADENHAM (9½ km, 6mi, 5.7cpm)
Follow 1-12. Then **13** R at road, L at main road. **A** Fork R along rough road for 80m, then R up steps and ½ L over field to stile just L of pole. **B** On to next stile. On up field to farm gate at far top corner. **C** Through gate & L in wood. Don't cross stile to road, but turn R over stile & up field by wood edge. Now follow 27 on.

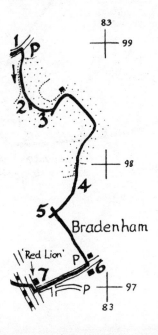

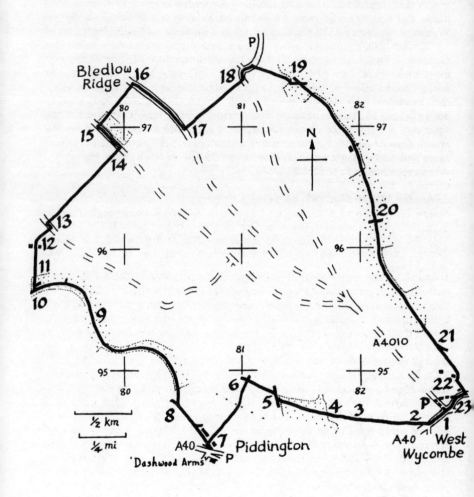

Bledlow Ridge **16**

18

19

15 80 · 97

17 81 ||

N

82 · 97

14

13

-12

96

96

20

11

10

9

21

A4010

95 · 80

81

95

82

22

6

8

5

4 **3**

P

2

23

1

½ km

¼ mi

7 Piddington

A40 West
Wycombe

A40

'Dashwood Arms' P

46

15   WEST OF WEST WYCOMBE (13km, 8mi, 5.1cpm)

After a good start up an open ridge, & a wooded section, you plunge down to a path along a 'bottom'. Then over two open & scenic ridges before returning along a mainly beech-wooded path on the ridge that ends at West Wycombe.

There may be muddy sections in the bottom (8-10).

West Wycombe is an attractive village with many old picturesque properties (around 16th Century). The house & grounds of nearby West Wycombe Park (built 1750-80) are also open to the public (National Trust).

Church Hill above the village, was the site of an Iron Age defended settlement. There was once a village on the hill, which has disappeared, leaving the Church of St. Lawrence, with its unusual interior, & golden ball. There is enough room inside the ball to hold a committee meeting, conduct a tortoise race, or do anything normally carried out in a small rectangular room (papering the walls could be tricky though. There is also a greater risk of being struck by lightning). Anything odd found in the district is almost certainly due to Sir Francis Dashwood (1708-1781) founder of the notorious Hell Fire Club. In the caves and passages excavated under the hill, there were diabolical goings on which reputable guide books are loath to reveal. To find out more you will have to sink to the level of the average tourist, bow to one of the few instances of commercialism in the Chilterns, & buy a ticket to the caves. All will then be revealed (so I am told). Club members ended up in the Mausoleum (built 1752).

PARK in the car park by the A4010 (826 947) 150m N of its junction with the A40 at W. Wycombe.

1 Return to the junction. Go SW 200m along A40 towards Oxford. 2 Then, near lane on L, go ½ R up 2 fields. 3 On up 3rd field (first with hedge on yr L) to stile at wood edge. 4 On in wood. 5 As wood ends, go 30m R along track, then L along track. 6 L along path towards middle 2 trees of a line of about 6 well spaced trees. Down (hedge on yr L) into farmyard. 7 On through small gate at once R through small gate & along path (long barn on yr R). Soon on along track. 8 At gates take R fork over field to gate & on in trees along valley bottom. 9 On through 2 gates. 10 30m before wood on R ends, go sharp R up path near wood edge to its top. 11 Here on up field (hedge on yr L) to farm. 12 On through farm & ⅓ R over field to road. 13 L along road 100m, then R along path down & up to road (fence on yr R). 14 L along road. 15 Go R up just inside edge of wood & on up to road (hedge on yr L). 16 R along road. 17 L along Scrubbs Lane & on down fields (hedge on yr R) to road. 18 On down road to bottom, the ½ R up field to path along its top edge. 19 On into wood at field's top corner & ½ R along track along ridge. 20 On over crossing track at end of pines. Later ignore a parallel track on yr R. 21 On over grass, passing L of the Golden Ball. Then bear R round trees to Mausoleum. 22 L down line of trees to road. 23 R along by road & over grass to car park or point 1.

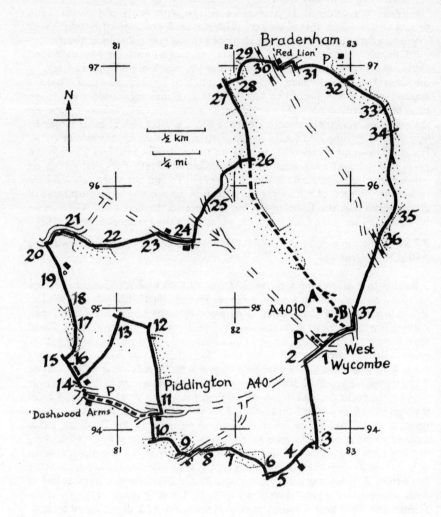

Bradenham

'Red Lion'

N

½ km

¼ mi

Piddington   A40

'Dashwood Arms'

West
Wycombe

A4010

16   WEST WYCOMBE TO BRADENHAM (12½ km, 7¾ mi, 6.5cpm)

Up a lane and through a series of small woods, reaching the valley near Piddington (11). Here up the other side and down to Ham Farm (14). Then up again through a wood, soon with good views. Over fields with wide views down to Chawley Farm, an Elizabethan building (24), and up to a wooded ridge (26). The ridge is left to drop down into Bradenham (31). Then along another wooded ridge (32-35) down to the road and up fields to the side of Church Hill above West Wycombe. Sometimes muddy at 19 for a short distance.

For notes on Bradenham see walk 14; on W. Wycombe see walk 15.

PARK in the car park by the A4010 (826 947) 150m N of its junction with the A40 at W. Wycombe.

1 Return to the junction. Go SW 200m along A40 towards Oxford. **2** Turn L up lane. **3** 50m before top fork R. **4** Near farm, go on to pass by pylon. **5** 100m on, take L fork along by hedge to gate. Through gate & R for 50m to stile in hedge. On over field. **6** On into wood. **7** On emerging, keep along hedge (on yr L) then beside wood (on yr R) until you come to stile. **8** Here go into wood. Soon out & L up road. **9** By farm fork ½ R along track. After 50m turn R over stile & down wood. Near wood bottom, path bears L. **10** Where path gets near wood edge, watch for stile at edge. Here go down field to house on road. **●11** R 100m along road, then L over main road & up track. **12** L along track just after passing top corner of wood. **13** L along path towards middle 2 trees of a line of about 6 widely spaced trees, & down (hedge on yr L) into farmyard. **14** On through small gate, at once R through small gate & along path (long barn on yr R). Soon on along track. **15** Watch for stile on R. Over, & up by hedge (on yr L) & **16** into wood. **17** On emerging, bear L to keep along wood edge & over stile. **18** Here ½ R to far corner of field. **19** On between pond and hedge, & along farm drive. **20** At road R, & very soon R again into field. Go along L edge of field. **21** Just after going R at field corner turn into wood along path (lane below on L). As lane turns L, the path goes on inside wood along its lower edge. Follow fence as it bears L to stile. **22** Here over fields towards farm with pylon behind it. **23** R at road. **24** L over stile opposite farm. The path crosses 2 small roads. **25** Climb hill up into wood. Path winds upwards. When it levels, cross over a wider track & keep on to a second cross track. **● 26** Here turn L. **27** At building, go R down beside fence for 100m. **28** Here L down to stile at wood edge. **29** Over & down to R corner of field. **30** Over railway to road. Here R 50m, L 150m, R 50m on roads. **31** Go L along stony track. **32** At sharp L bend (5m before signpost) go on in same direction as before bend (SE) up narrow path. At fence go through. Keep on along track among beeches. (At first track is not clear. Follow arrows). Ignore path turning L off yours. **33** Ignore cross track. Further on path climbs gently to within 20m of wood edge. **34** Here meet another track & go ½ R along it. Follow arrow straight on where a track forks ½ L. **35** When path reaches wood end it goes ½ R down by fence (on yr L) to railway. **36** On to road & on up to far corner of field. **37** Here go down road & soon R along road. (Short cut over grass to reach P).

16A   SHORTER WALK (9km, 5½ mi, 5.5cpm)

Follow 1 to 10, then L along road, soon forking R. R at road end, to cross A40 & ½ L up track soon passing long barn on yr R. Now follow 15 to 25, then R along track. (Later ignore parallel track on yr R). **A** Near Golden Ball, go on across grass to pass it to the L & bear R round trees to Mausoleum. **B** L down line of trees to road. R along road back to start.   **49**

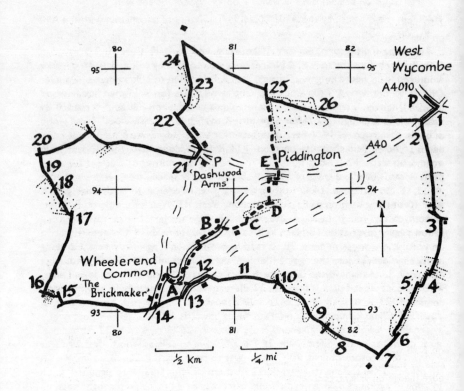

17 WEST WYCOMBE TO WHEELEREND (12km, 7½ mi, 5.3cpm)

At first you pass through woods and hills of the West Wycombe Estate, making use of some new paths. After Wheelerend Common there is a beautiful open ridge (16-17) before a valley path leads to Piddington. Yet more views on the final climb of the day to a grand ridge with a fine wood and one of the best descents of the district.

PARK in the car park by the A4010 (826 947) 150m N of its junction with the A40 at W. Wycombe.

1 Return to the junction. Go SW 200m along A40 towards Oxford. **2** Then turn L up lane. Bear L at top. **3** By thatched cottage, go R over stile and on by hedge on yr L. **4** At bottom, over stile in fence and R along field edge. Go L at its corner. **5** After 100m go R to wood at arrow. Soon faint path reaches track. Go L along it. **6** Out of wood and R up track (hedge on yr R). **7** R over stile before farm (hedge on yr L). **8** On into wood and out by stiles. Over field. **9** Into wood. Follow arrows, soon down by wire fence on yr R. At bottom, on up for 100m. **10** When path bends R, make for nearby metal gate and stile. Over stile and up field. **11** Aim for gate and stile in front of barns. Over stile and ½ R to road just R of barn. **12** L along road. ●**13** After road bends L and descends, turn R along grass track in bracken. It bears L to white post (memorial) to L of phone box. **14** Over road and along lane. **15** 100m after lane turns R, you go ½ L over stile to wood. At stile go on in wood. On across gap in wood. **16** On leaving wood go R along track. **17** At wood corner go L. Enter wood after 10m at arrow. Ignore rough track forking L after 50m, & crossing paths. **18** At bottom, on up (wood on yr L). **19** At top, leave edge and go ½ R to stile. **20** Here, R down valley bottom track. **21** L at lane, over main road and ½ L along track (barns on yr R). **22** At stile (hidden in hedge) go R up into wood. **23** On leaving wood, go L by its edge to reach a fine view. **24** Here, up field towards farm and sharp R along field edge. Soon on along track. ●**25** Bear R when track comes in on L. Soon L into wood. **26** On over field to its corner. On down to road. L along road (or, to continue walk, go R along lane and follow 3 onwards).

17A SHORTER WALK (8km, 5mi, 7.2cpm)

Follow 1-12, then ½ R along stony track. **A** Soon R along Piddington Lane. Over stile on R to walk beside lane. Over 2 stiles & walk beside lane (now on yr R). **B** Over stile by house & R over lane & along track passing L of farm. Soon, on along field edge (hedge on yr R) to corner. Through gate, then L down to wood. **C** Follow path down wood to lower edge, then R 50m to stile. **D** L over stile & field to gate just L of single house. **E** R 80m & L over main road & on up track. **25** At top corner of wood, turn R into wood & follow 26.

17B AROUND PIDDINGTON (8½ km, 5¼ mi, 4.2cpm)

At Wheelerend Common (804 933) go SW along road past The Brickmaker & ½ R along lane. Follow 15-24, then bear R when track comes in on L. **E** On over road, R 80m along minor road & L (just after house) up field to stile at wood edge. **D** At stile, fork R along path in wood (near edge) for 50m. Here turn L up path to top wood corner. **C** Here, over stile and up 50m (hedge on yr R) to gate. Here R along field edge (hedge on yr L). Near houses, go on through gate (between hedges) to lane. **B** Over lane & L over stile. Walk by lane, then cross it by 2 stiles & walk beside lane (now on yr R). Over stile & on along lane to common.

18 HUGHENDEN (11½ km, 7mi, 6cpm)

There are views of the Hughenden Valley as you cross it to Cryers Hill and come back to Hughenden Manor (National Trust) the home of Disraeli. Part of this is now a museum containing his pictures, books, furniture, etc. He is buried in a vault at the little Church nearby.

Next through woods and fields to Downley Common. Down Blacksmith's Lane, later with views, to West Wycombe. Here the Pedestal (1752) is an odd signpost which does not name the three towns to which the roads lead (after reading page 47 you can guess who was responsible). You see more good views before the final flat mile.

Expect some mud in damper seasons at 9, 13, 22, 29.

PARKING. Leave the A4128 3km (2mi) N of High Wycombe at a roundabout. Take minor road N and soon turn L up the hill towards Naphill. At the top, where road bends R, go on along a lane to its end (848 962).

1 Walk back (NE) along lane. At road junction, go on down road. 2 Soon after it bends R go L (30m after drive) down path in field. 3 Over stile by wood edge and down between fences. On down rough road. 4 At bottom R 50m, & L over field. 5 Up drive. 6 Fork R up stony track for 50m & then R between fences. Up into wood. 7 At field follow path beside fence (on yr R). 8 Follow rough drive to road. 9 Cross road & bear R at footpath sign. Go on along top edge of field. 10 On in next field. Keep just below shrubs. 11 Through gate at field corner & down enclosed path. 12 Out into field then R 70m & L along edge of this field. 13 At far end R down bridlepath. 14 L at road for 50m, then R along drive & on grass to pass just L of house & Church. ● 15 Up to cattle grid sign. Here go up drive. 16 Just past

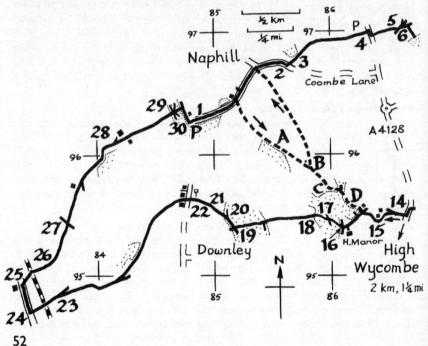

52

Hughenden Manor, where drive bends L, go on **down** path which at once bears R. 17 Keep on down where path crosses yours. 18 Out of wood & over field. On into wood. 19 At wide cross track, turn up R. 20 Soon at fork keep on L main track. 21 At open common, keep forward on rising track (NW) to playing field. Make for group of houses behind it. 22 At road, find & go along track starting between a house & old Smithy (opposite bus stop). 23 On under railway. 24 R at road. 25 By buildings, go ½ R over field to gate & under railway. On up field (fence on yr L). 26 Bear ½ L with fence. 27 At bottom, on over track & up to barn. On along farm road. 28 Fork R to pass farm on yr L. 29 Where lane stops being surfaced, go on 100m to a track. Here turn R (hedge on yr L). 30 Soon after house (on yr L), go L along surfaced lane.

18A HUGHENDEN & WEST WYCOMBE (8km, 5mi, 5.4cpm)

I Walk back (NE) along lane. After lane starts climbing, turn sharp R (by Oakwood House) over fields by hedge (on yr R). **A** At dip, where wood on yr R bears R, keep on over field to far corner stile just R of large tree. **B** Over stile & R along by hedge (on yr R). **C** At wood, go ½ L 100m to field corner & on into wood. Soon along wood edge. **D** Go ½ L when fence (on yr L) bends L. At drive, go up it & follow 16-30.

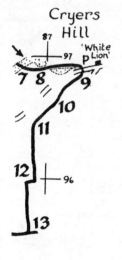

Cryers Hill

18B HUGHENDEN & CRYERS HILL (6km, 3¾ mi, 5.6cpm)

PARKING. Leave the A4128 3km (2mi) N of High Wycombe at a roundabout. Take minor road N and park in the rough Trees Road, the 3rd turning on yr L.

Follow main walk from 4 to 14. Then up to cattlegrid sign. Here go up path just to L of Park Cottage. **D** Soon emerge from trees & go ½ R by fence (on yr R) along wood edge. Into wood (ignore path going off R 50m before you leave wood). Out of wood & ½ L along its edge. **C** By stile turn ½ R along hedge (on yr L). Sharp R down road. Now follow 2 & 3.

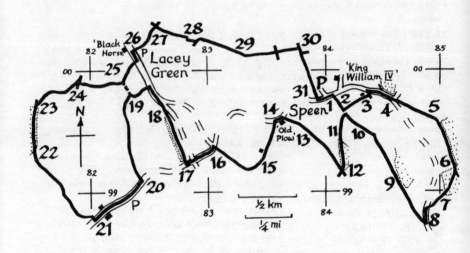

'Black Horse
82
00
25
26
27 X
28
Lacey
Green
83
29
30
84
85
00
'King
William IV'
P
31
2
3
4
5
Speen
1
24
19
18
14
13
11
10
6
N
17
16
15
12 X
9
82
7
99
20
½ km
8
P
83
99
¼ mi
84
21
22
23

19 AROUND SPEEN (12km, 7½ mi, 5.3cpm)

Soon after leaving the village, there are magnificent views near Upper North Dean (8). Further ups and downs bring you to a short flat section near Grim's Ditch (17). It is probably Saxon and its purpose is uncertain. Then comes a gentle descent, followed by the splendid ridge climb of Callows Hill (22) and further views on the return to Speen.

There can be short muddy sections at 5 and 30.

PARK at Speen in quiet side road e.g. Studridge Lane (840 998) N of the main road through the village.

1 From the main road go SE along Water Lane. 2 On over 2 stiles & L to field corner. On down next field to corner stile. 3 On down path, & over garden to track. Here L to road & R down road. 4 At Spring Coppice Lane ½ L over stile & up field. On over stile to far top corner of field. 5 Here ⅓ R along track 60m, then on along field edge (wood on yr L). 6 On into wood 70m, then take R fork down. 7 Leave wood at stile. On down by hedge. 8 L along road. At phone box, sharp R along track. On up fields by hedge (& later wood) on yr R. 9 Bear L away from wood edge to stile 40m from it. Here on along ridge by fence on yr R. 10 On where fence stops. At hedge go L along it (keep it on yr R). 11 On down into wood. 12 At bottom, over stile & R along field edge (hedge on yr R). Later, path switches to R of fence & is slightly above valley bottom. 13 Watch for field gate. Here cross stile by it & go to far field corner. 14 L up road & L just after Plough Inn. Up edge of field & through Horses' Rest Home. 15 Leave Home by main drive (between fences). 16 At road turn L. On over main road for 70m. 17 Here R along field edge. 18 On along road. L along Church Lane for 200m. ● 19 Here L between hedges. Over 2 stiles & on between hedge & fence. On down valley to gate. 20 R along road. 21 100m after farm, go R over stile for 30m, then L up grass track, soon with hedge on yr R. 22 On into wood. 23 Out of wood. Follow hedge on yr R as it bears R to stile & (further on) to track. Down track. 24 At bottom, sharp R 20m, then L down gap in hedge & straight up field (aim just R of house). On over next field 100m to gate & stile. 25 Along drive. L along lane. L at road 50m, then 26 R along Kiln Lane. 27 Where it narrows at a mini cross roads, turn R. Keep on with hedge on yr R. 28 When near farm gate, watch for stile in hedge. Over this & L to stile on to farm track (concrete). Here L along track which at once bears R. 29 Where concrete track ends, go ½ L down between fences to bottom & on up. 30 R along track. 31 At road, go L.

19A SHORTER WALK (9km, 5½ mi, 4.7cpm)

Follow 1-18. Carry on along lane to main road. Here turn L & follow 26-31.

19B SHORTER WALK (9km, 5½ mi, 5.1cpm)

Go SE along Water Lane, then over stile & R along hedge (on yr R). Now follow 11-31.

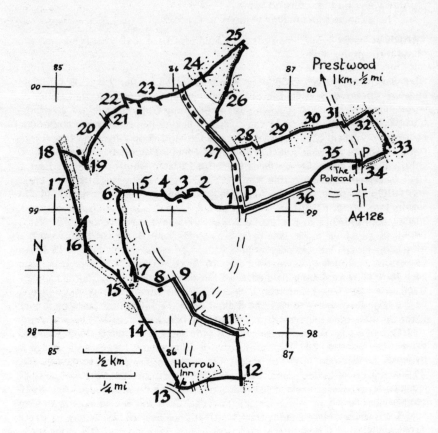

Prestwood
1 km, ½ mi

The Polecat

A4128

N

½ km
¼ mi

Harrow
Inn

20 SOUTH EAST OF SPEEN (12½ km, 7¾ mi, 7.1cpm)

Six ups and downs make this a walk of ever changing views, with some short sections of pleasant woodland. Pretty free of mud problems, but a bull was once sighted on the path between 13 and 14.

PARK in car park (866 991) just N of minor road junction reached by leaving the A4128 and turning W 1.5 km (1mi) S of Prestwood.

1 From car park go L along road & soon R up field edge. 2 Over stile near top & on, bearing L along field edge to its corner. 3 Here go L to drive & R along it, at once forking along the L of 2 drives & soon passing to R of white house. 4 100m after drive bends R turn ½ L at stile and go down to field corner. 5 Over road and up into wood. 6 Here take L fork. Follow arrows along path parallel to wood edge. ● 7 Fork L on smaller path & soon (30m before end of wood) go ½ L to stile & down field towards house. 8 Through 2 metal gates just L of House. Follow wood fence down to next gate. Through gate & down drive. 9 R along road. 10 On at crossroads. 11 At wood turn R up field. On over stile. 12 R at crosspath, soon going down in wood. On through houses to Harrow Inn. 13 At road go R 20m then through gate (near post box) & over large field towards wood. 14 Over stile. On up past 2 clumps of trees. Into wood at stile. 15 Bear slightly L along path (at first near wood edge). 16 Go ½ R up drive. 200m later, sharp L at footpath sign. Soon sharp R along top edge of wood. 17 On over field (wood on yr R). 18 At track, go sharp R across wood to edge stile. On over field to stile just R of house. Follow drive to lane. 19 At once L into wood. Down L edge of wood. 20 Down by hedge to road. 21 L at road. At bus stop go R up path. 22 At top go L 50m along farm track then sharp R. Go L along track just before road reaches buildings. 23 At 2 gates leave track & go on down field (hedge on yr R) to road ● & up into wood. 24 In wood go on up path (vague at first). On over wider track (soon, ignore path going down R). 25 Over stile at wood edge & R 10m. Over stile & R along wood edge. 26 On down drive to road. Here L. 27 At footpath sign ½ L to field corner. Into wood & up by fence. 28 50m from top, go ½ R to stile at wood edge. Cross field by fence. 29 On into wood, along edge. 30 On by hedge & along track to road. 31 R along road 50m, then L. 32 R at field corner (keep inside wood). 33 When you see small hollow on yr L, fork R along small path soon by wood edge. Go R over stile & on by line of trees to road. 34 R along road, L over The Polecat car park & over stile. ⅓ R to corner stile. 35 Down field to its lowest point. 36 Here down road. R at bottom. (To continue walk go L up field edge & follow 2 onwards.)

20A SHORTER WALK (9½ km, 6mi, 6.5cpm)

Follow 1-6. 7 Fork L on smaller path to stay just inside wood. 15 At stile carry on inside wood (at first near its edge). Follow 16-36.

20B SHORTER WALK (9km, 5½ mi, 6.7cpm)

Follow 1-22. Follow 23, but at road go R, back to start.

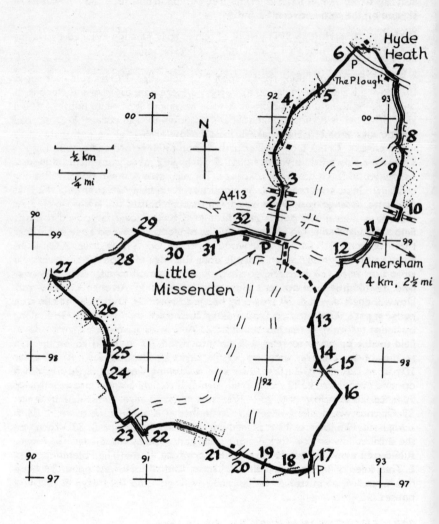

Hyde
Heath

6
7
P
'The Plough'
92 4
5
93
00
00
8
9
3
A413
2
P
32
10
29
11
1
28 30 31
P
12
27
Amersham
4 km, 2½ mi
Little
Missenden
13
26
14
15
25
24
92
16
23 P
22
21 19 18 17
20
P

½ km
¼ mi

N

91
90
99
00
99
98
98
92
90
91
93
97
97

21 LITTLE MISSENDEN (11½ km, 7¼ mi, 4cpm)

One of the gentler walks which just managed to get into the book. Save it for a hot day when you don't feel like trudging up steep ridges. You may find the shorter walk better than the longer one, which starts with a brief pleasant valley view before an easy wooded climb (mainly in pines) to the plateau of Hyde Heath. After leaving the village, you soon pass down a fine beech wood and fields back to Little Missenden. Then a gentle shady climb to another flat section (14-20) before more gentle contours are met. The final ridge path makes a good ending to both walks.

The village is attractive and unspoilt, and the Saxon Church contains some remarkable 13th century wall paintings.

PARK near Little Missenden church (921 990).

I Go over stile just L of church & on along field edge. **2** On over road, up field to bridge. **3** Over it & on 10m, then ½ L up grassy track in wood. Ignore crossing tracks. **4** At fork go R. **5** On over cross track to wood edge. On along field edge. **6** Over road & on along path that at once turns R to reach track (50m R of house). On over this track, soon bearing R off path to reach open field. On over field to pass The Plough. **7** R along Brays Lane. **8** On down Chalk Lane 100m, then L over stile into wood for 20m, & ½ R down path. **9** At wood edge, go on over stile, along field edge to bridge. **10** Over this & R. At stile go L along field edge to road. **11** Here R 50m, then L over main road & on down lane. **12** 100m after lane bends ½ R, turn L along stony track. **13** Ignore path into wood. **14** When path turns ½ R, you go L over stile, then ½ R over field to hedge gap. **15** Here go on to far corner of field. **16** Here ½ R over stile & along by hedge (on yr L) to lane just L of farm. **17** On along lane 80m, then R over field to stile near nearest pole in field. (Ignore path going ⅔ R). **18** On to short section of wood fence with stile. **19** On by hedge to road. **20** Here ½ L for 20m, then ½ R along field edge. **21** ⅓ R down to wood corner, through wood & on up to road. **22** Along short road, then R along road, L along main road for 70m. **23** Here R along path, over stile & on to far L corner of field, passing just R of jutting out hedge corner. **24** Over stile & along by hedge (on yr L) to corner stile. **25** Here on over drive & along the R of 2 parallel paths. **26** Where the 2 paths join, go ½ R down stony path. **27** Sharp R along farm drive, then ⅓ R between wood fences. **28** Over stile & down by hedge (on yr L) until it turns L. Then keep on up to ridge path. **29** R down this path. **30** Through hedge gap & ⅓ L over field soon with hedge on yr L. **31** Over track & on to stile just L of houses. **32** On along road.

21A SHORTER WALK (7½ km, 4¾ mi, 4cpm)

At the church go E along road 50m & R along road to junction. Here ½ L over field past tree to shady track & ½ R up it. Now follow 13-32.

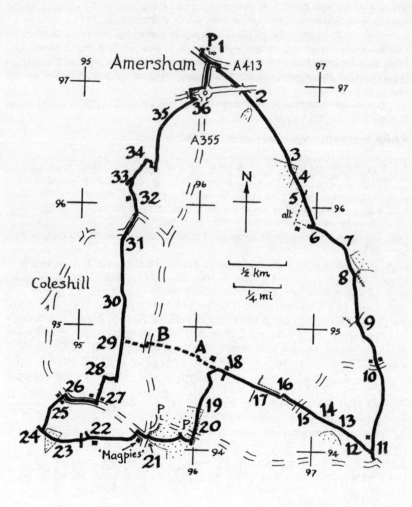

Amersham

A413

A355

N

½ km
¼ mi

Coleshill

B
A

'Magpies'

22 SOUTH FROM AMERSHAM (11½ km, 7¼ mi, 4.5cpm)

The walk starts with a splendid climb out of the Misbourne valley, followed by a passage across gently undulating fields, seldom without a view. Near Coleshill, there is a level section until the final descent of an open ridge.

There may be a little mud near farms e.g. at 10, 22.

Amersham is a beautiful old market town with many 17th century buildings lining the wide main street. These include the Town Hall (with its open arcade, once used as a market), the original Grammar School, almshouses and several coaching inns. Parts of St. Mary's Church are 13th century and there are 15th century brasses and memorials inside. There is also a lovely 18th century Baptist Chapel.

PARK in Amersham car park 100m W of the A413/A355 junction (960 972).

1 At junction go along A413 away from Amersham. After 50m go R 10m, then L along track under road to gate. 2 Here go ⅓ R up fields to the L hand edge of wood. 3 Into wood at stile. 4 On out of wood towards distant pylon. 5 At hedge corner go on over field (or round its edge if path is missing). 6 Follow hedge (kept on yr R) to stile 50m before wood. 7 R over stile & L to fence corner near far end of wood. 8 Here go ½ R (S) over field under cables to stile in hedge. 9 ½ L over stile & down fields, soon with hedge on yr R, to farm. 10 On over road. Soon up stony track (hedge on yr R). 11 After passing house, track goes L. Here turn sharp R over stile along path. 12 Over stile & on along field edge (fence on yr R). 13 On down & up field to stile by group of trees (or keep by field edge). 14 On past old stile, with fence on yr R. 15 On over road (hedge on yr L). 16 Near field corner, go L over stile, then R (hedge on yr R). 17 At hedge T-junction, go on over stile. ● 18 Just after passing house, go on over stile & ½ L across small field to stile in hedge. Over & L to follow edge of field along to wood. 19 On along track in wood to road. 20 On over road. Follow track as it soon bears R & gently descends. 50m before it returns to road, go ⅓ L along path (marked by low posts). 21 At road go L 20m & R 100m along side road. Then L up track. 22 At farm, leave track & go on over stile, over cross track & on along field edge (hedge on yr R). 23 On in wood (bearing slightly R) to far edge. 24 On out of wood 30m, then R through iron gate (fence on yr L). 25 Over stile & ⅓ R (ENE) over field to stile (between houses) & out to road. 26 R along road. 27 L just before 2nd house on L. Soon along edge of 2 fields (hedge on yr L). 28 Over stile & R (hedge on yr R) 100m, then L (fence on yr L). 29 Keep on (fence on yr R). 30 Over stile & on by hedge (on yr R) to road. 31 Here go on until road goes R, then ½ L down path. 32 At field go along L edge. After slight rise, you reach a bank which separates 2 fields. 33 Go R along bottom of bank. 34 At end of bank turn R to valley bottom & R 50m. Here go L up to track & L along it, soon down valley bottom. 35 On beside gardens until you see wood gap in barbed fence. Go L over it & R along field edge. 36 At field corner, turn L along path, cross bridge, go R to roundabout and L down road.

22A SHORTER WALK (9km, 5½ mi, 4.5cpm)

Follow 1-17, then after passing house, go on over stiles (several). **A** After rough area go R over stile & L along field edge (hedge on yr L). **B** At road go a short way L, then R down bank & up field. Soon go R along path & follow 30 to 36.

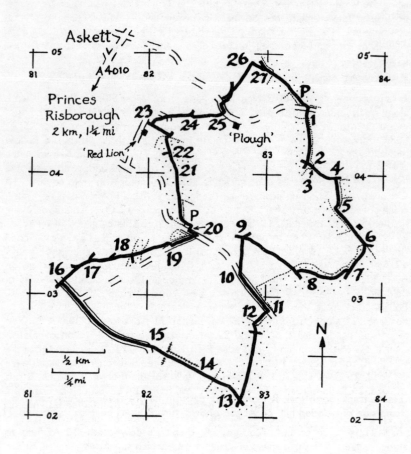

Askett

81 05   82 05   84 05

A 4010

Princes
Risborough
2 km, 1¼ mi

'Red Lion'

26

27

P

23

24 25   1

'Plough'

2 4

83   3

04   5   04

22

21   6

P

20 9

18   7

19 10 8

16   11

17   03

12

15   13

14   N

81 02   82 02   84 02

½ km

¼ mi

23   WHITELEAF HILL (10½ km, 6½ mi, 5.7cpm)

The walk consists of many wooded and open sections, reaching a climax with a fine climb up to Whiteleaf Hill, followed by an attractive finale through the Nature Reserve below Pulpit Hill.

There may be a few muddy patches (1-2, 11-12) so it is best to avoid tackling this in a damp season.

The chalk cross near the summit of Whiteleaf Hill, like the markings at Bledlow and Watlington, is not very old. There is no evidence they date any earlier than 18th century. The chalk lion near Whipsnade I judge to be 20th century.

PARKING. Leave the A4010 at Askett roundabout (NE of Princes Risborough). After 2 km (1¼ mi) use car park (833 046) near Pulpit Hill.

1 Turn L out of car park (E) along road & at once R down path. 2 At small dip go L up path to stile. 3 On by hedge (on yr R). 4 At wood corner, go R along its edge. 5 At field corner go L along next field edge (wood on yr R) to farm. On down drive. 6 At bottom, go R up clear track. 7 Turn R (before losing sight of wood edge) along small path marked by arrow. Path keeps near wood edge. 8 At path junction bear R, so leaving wood 50m later (hedge on yr R). 9 At drive turn L through iron gate over field (hedge on yr L at first) to gate. 10 L along road. 11 At wood on R, turn R along path just outside wood. 12 At field corner turn L along track in wood (fence on yr L). 13 Turn R along crossing path (arrows on tree), first in pines, then down in beeches. 14 On over fields to road. 15 On along road. 16 R along Upper Icknield Way. 17 At fork, go R up field by fence on yr R to stile at wood edge. 18 On up path with steps. Soon over stile & on up field passing just to R of the nearest bushes, to reach stile. 19 Here, on up road & L at junction. 20 Soon turn R into car park & at once L. At end of car park, go on along track for 50m. Then go ½ R keeping near fence on yr R (at first field on yr R) to reach clearing at top of hill. 21 Here ½ L to go gently down path. 22 Ignore path going L where descent steepens. Bear R along fence. 20m before road, go sharp L down path. 23 50m before road, go R for 50m, then ½ R between fences to road. Here ½ R up road & across in front of pavilion to gate on its L. On down golf course. 24 Through gap in tall hedges & along path to road. 25 L down road 80m, then R along path which soon runs beside track. Soon fork R along small path up nature reserve. Aim towards L hand side of wooded hill. 26 At top of field, turn R along edge to its corner. 27 Then ½ L over tree roots to main track.

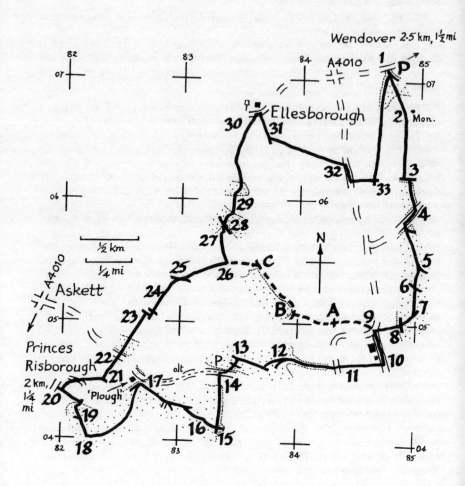

Wendover 2·5 km, 1½ mi

A4010

Ellesborough

Mon.

Askett

½ km
¼ mi

A4010

Princes
Risborough

2 km,
¼
mi

'Plough'

alt

N

24   COOMBE & WHITELEAF HILLS (12½ km, 7¾ mi, 6.1cpm)

After a steep climb to Coombe Hill (2) there is a fine ridge to walk along, first with good views, and then through woods. Then through more fine woods, East to Whiteleaf Hill (18). A classic return route over golf course and downland (Nature Reserve 23-25) to Ellesborough (30) and over fields and along the foot of Coombe Hill.

From 14-15 can be muddy. If necessary reach 17 by road.

The shorter walks pass as near as you can get to Chequers, an Elizabethan country house now kept for the use of the Prime Minister. Once the path passed by some large deadly nightshade plants — did the authorities have the path moved in case someone was tempted to poison the P.M? Anyway, keep to the footpath•or you might get arrested.

PARK by A4010 at the foot of Coombe Hill (847 071), ½ km (¼ mi) E of the cross-road near Ellesborough.

1 At road sign 'Ellesborough' (on A4010 from Wendover) (847 072) turn S off road towards Coombe Hill. Ignore L fork. Go through gate and **then** fork L up Hill. 2 At monument, ½ R along a nearly level path with gorse and shrubs on yr L. 3 L at a crossing fence and soon R over stile and along top wood edge. 4 At road go R along it for 100m. Then L along track parallel to wood edge and 30m from its edge. 5 At fork take R path (path winds about but keeps in same general direction, S). 6 When path gently descends, follow arrows to cross other tracks. 7 On reaching a clearer track running down to corner of a large field (100m away), go R down it. 8 At corner ⅓ R between 2 fields to road. ● 9 L along road past farm. 10 Just after last house, go R over field to road. 11 Here, L 10m then R (keep fence on yr L) up into strip of trees and later into wood. 12 On over clearing into wood and ½ R along wider path. 13 After 200m turn L along path. On over stile and track. 14 R along road and soon L along track. 15 At a small dip go R beside a fence (on yr R). 16 ½ R down sunken path to valley bottom. On down valley bottom to The Plough. 17 Just before The Plough, go L up track. At once fork L up ridge. 18 At top of hill go ½ R (NNW) gently down. 19 Where descent gets steep, ignore path going L and soon bear R along fence. 20m before road, go sharp L down path. 20 50m before road go R for 50m, then ½ R between fences to road. Here ½ R up road and across in front of pavilion to gate on its L. On down golf course. 21 ½ L to keep by tall hedge (on yr R) down to road. 22 Over road and on up path, then on over field. 23 At far field edge go on 10m through shrubs, R along path for 50m, L for 20m to stile, and on in same direction over stile (fence on yr R). 24 On down where fence turns R. Then up to stile. 25 On up steps, ½ R up track for 30m to stile. Over stile and on over grass soon by fence (on yr L) to pass by top of deep valley, & up to gate. ● 26 At gate go L over stile and along by fence (on yr R). 27 Down to and over stile. Now along fence on yr L and up to stile by gate. 28 On over drive, through wood and over field. 29 Down among dark box trees, and then on over chalk grassland and down field to Church. 30 R along road and soon R again along track. 31 At hedge gap, go ½ L across field to road. 32 R along road 100m, then L along track up to wood. 33 Here L along wood edge to road.

24A   COOMBE HILL (7½ km, 4¾ mi, 5.3cpm)

Follow 1-8, then on over road and field, past pole and slightly L to cross drive and 3 stiles. **A** Here on over field to stile. **B** Over stile and R along track, over stile and along wood edge to stile. **C** Over stile and ½ L over field to gate. Here go R along fence (keeping it on yr R). Then follow 27.

24B   WHITELEAF HILL (7½ km, 4¾ mi, 6cpm)

PARK near Pulpit Hill as for walk 23.

Turn L out of car park (E) along road and R at once down path. Follow 15 to 25. Then at gate, go ½ R over field to stile. **C** Here ½ R along wood edge, over stile by gate and curve round to next stile. **B** Here, L down field to cross 3 stiles and drive. **A** On past pole and slightly R to stile at road. Here ½ R up road past farm. Then follow 10-14.

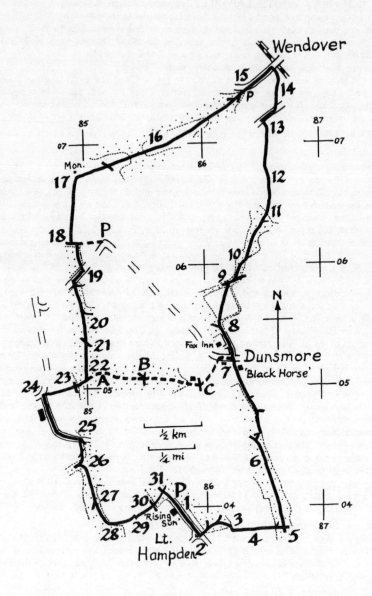

Wendover

15
14
P
13
16
85
07
87
07
Mon.
17
12
11
18
P
10
19
9
06
06
N
20
8
21
Fox Inn
22
B
Dunsmore
23
A
7
'Black Horse'
24
05
05
25
½ km
¼ mi
26
31
P
27
30
1
86
28
29
Rising Sun
04
04
Lt.
3
87
Hampden
2
4
5
6

25 COOMBE HILL & LITTLE HAMPDEN (11½ km, 7¼ mi, 5.6cpm)

Starting at Little Hampden and passing its tiny Church with a two storey timber 15th century porch, the walk encounters a fine selection of beech woods and views before reaching the outskirts of Wendover. (With a little extra walking, this can be the start of walks 25 or 25A). It is a pleasant town with some 16th century houses and thatched cottages. South of the town there is the 14th century Church, which has an interesting brass memorial). Then comes the splendid ridge climb to Coombe Hill, followed by magnificent views, before a return through more woodlands.

There may be the odd muddy section. Paths are rather vague at 20, 21.

PARK at Little Hampden at the end of its road (857 040).

1 Walk back (SE) along road. **2** At end of grass triangle, go L along track into wood. Soon fork R down off main track. Soon fork R again to reach bottom corner of wood. **3** On leaving wood, turn R along hedge for 30m to gate, then L down field edge. **4** Up 2nd field (hedge on yr L) and on steeply up in wood. **5** L along clear level path near top of rise. Path stays roughly 80m from top edge of wood, with fairly steep ground on yr L. **6** Fork R up path off track for 40m to stile. Over & R 30m, then L along path just inside wood (at first). ● **7** On over road. **8** Soon after road ends go on (not ½ L). At field go across between fences. **9** Into wood. At narrow clearing go ½ L down its L side by iron fence (on yr L). On into wood. **10** Soon after descent go ½ L up path (ignore small path down). Fork L to stile 50m before reaching edge of wood. **11** Out of wood and ½ L across field. **12** Over stile and ⅓ L up field. Over stile and on between fences. **13** R along road and ½ L across field at first gap. **14** At field edge, ½ L between fence and hedge, then L along road. **15** On up track when road bears R. Soon take R fork. Soon fork L (acorn sign) and shortly go up steps. **16** Through short section of wood & then climb gently on to monument. **17** Here go L along nearly level path with slope & view on yr R. ● **18** Turn L beside crossing fence. Soon R over stile and along wood edge. **19** R along road for 100m. Then L along track parallel to wood edge and 30m from its edge. **20** At fork, take R path. (It winds about but keeps roughly the same direction). **21** When path gently descends, follow arrows to cross over other tracks. ● **22** At clear track, go down it 100m to field corner. **23** Here, ⅓ R between 2 fields. **24** L along lane past farm. **25** When lane enters wood, turn R off it. Soon over stile and along enclosed path. **26** Turn L along path. **27** Take L fork. **28** When path leaves wood, go R beside hedge to field corner. **29** Here, R 5m, then L (ENE) along field edge (hedge on yr L). **30** On over track onto wood. **31** R along track.

25A COOMBE HILL (8km, 5mi, 5.6cpm)

PARKING. Go NW through Dunsmore. After 1.5km (1mi), park where road turns L (852 062).

Walk W (½ L relative to road from Dunsmore) by fence to stile. Here L over stile and along wood edge. Follow 19-21, then at clear track (22) go sharp L up it. **A** Bear R with track along edge of clearing (on yr L). **B** On, where paths meet. **C** At end of track, on up field over 3 stiles and bear ⅓ L to 4th stile. On up to house. **7** At road, R 80m, then L along lane. Now follow 8-17, and turn L beside crossing fence (18).

25B LITTLE HAMPDEN (6½ km, 4¼ mi, 6.1cpm)

Follow 1-6, then L along road for 80m and ½ L over stile down field. Watch for stile in fence ahead. Over this and down to buildings over 3 more stiles. **C** On up track. **B** at fork, take L (main) track, first with clearing on yr L, then on yr R. **A** Bear L with track as you reach end of clearing. After descent to wood edge follow 23-31.

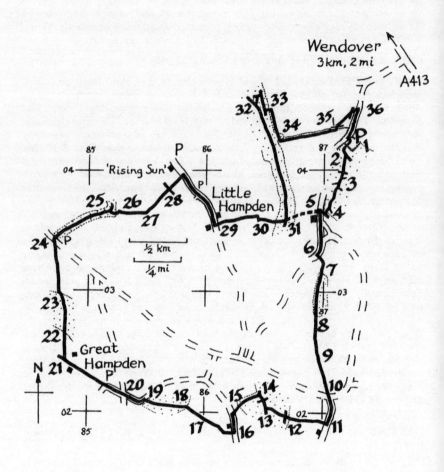

Wendover
3km, 2mi
A413

'Rising Sun'

Little
Hampden

P

½ km
¼ mi

24

23

22

N 21

Great
Hampden
P

20 19
18
17 16 13 12 11
15 14
10

9

8

7

6

5 4

3

2 1

P

36
35
34
32 33

25 26
27 28
29 30 31

26 THE HAMPDENS (11km, 6¾ mi, 5.2cpm)

A quieter gentler walk away from the popular Coombe Hill, but still plenty of fine views mingled with attractive woodland. Don't get lost at the start — there are many paths in Cockshoots Wood. The tiny Church at Little Hampden has a two-storied 15th century porch.

There can be the odd short muddy section (e.g. 4, 16).

PARKING. Go along Cobblershill Lane, a turning off the A413, 3km (2mi) S from Wendover. Park in the wood (872 042).

1 Go on (SW) parallel to road along track soon bearing L. 2 When it straightens, leave it ½ R up path marked by arrows. 3 Ignore crossing path and side turnings. 4 R along track at edge of wood. 5 L along road. 6 After road bends to R, turn L along track for 50m. Then R along field edge. 7 On in wood. 8 On along field edge (hedge on yr R). 9 Through gap near field corner and ⅓ L down field to road junction. 10 On up lane. 11 Watch for footpath sign and go R. Path goes along bottom edge of fields to wood. 12 On in wood. Path goes gently down, soon crossing track, then into pines. 13 Soon after leaving pines, path reaches track. Turn R down it. 14 Ignore track that crosses it, but 50m further on at field corner turn L along path just inside wood. 15 Over stile, across field by fence to road and L along it. 16 Just after farm turn R through farm gates and along field edge (farm fence on yr R). At field corner, ½ R through gate. 50m later, ½ L along track between fences. 17 On through gate to wood. 18 Follow path in wood. 19 At road, go L along it. 20 On over cross road. Soon, on along drive where road bends L. 21 Just past buildings, go through white gate, and at once ⅔ R through another gate across field to stile. 22 Here enter pines. On at next stile down wood. 23 At wood bottom on over field to its corner. 24 Over road and through gate opposite. 25 When track turns L, go R 10m to stile and ⅓ R up field to stile in hedge. 26 Up by fence. 27 At stile, ⅓ L over large field to gap in hedge. (Gap is a bit nearer R corner of field than L.) 28 Through gap and on to road. R along road. 29 Go L just after Manor Farm. Follow hedge on yr L down field and up. 30 At wood, ½ L up track, soon between fences. ● 31 Near top, at stiles, turn L along level path. Path stays roughly 80m from top of wood, with fairly steep ground on yr L. 32 Fork R up path off track for 40m to stile. Over & R 30m, then R along path just inside wood. 33 Turn L at white arrow, along path 50m to wood edge. Over stile & R along field edge. 34 Over stile & L down fields with hedge on yr L. 35 150m before bottom, where hedge on L joins yours, go L over track & ½ R to stiles & road. 36 R along road.

26 SHORTER WALK (8½ km, 5¼ mi, 5.1cpm)

PARK at Little Hampden at the end of its road (857 040).

Walk back (SE) along road. Follow 29 & 30. Go on out of wood, over field past farm & R along road. Follow 6 to 28.

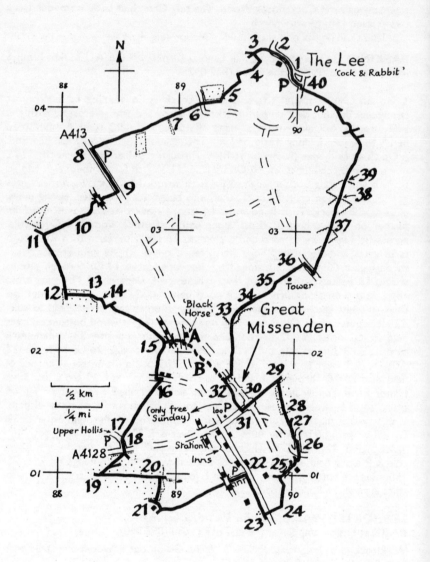

The Lee
'Cock & Rabbit'

A413

P

'Black Horse'

Great Missenden

A

B

Tower

'only free Sunday'

loo P

Upper Hollis

A4128

Station

Inns

½ km

¼ mi

27 AROUND GREAT MISSENDEN (13.5km, 8½ mi, 4.7cpm)

Starting at The Lee on the flat, but soon on an open path down the valley and up the other side. Then an attractive descent (11-15). Next the walk skirts Great Missenden with a variety of woods and views, before finally climbing back to the plateau.

In damp seasons, there will be some muddy patches.

The old coaching inn, 'The George', in Great Missenden dates from 1480. The Church above the town, has a Norman font. 'Missenden Abbey' is not an abbey, but is built on the site of one founded in 1133. The Lee is a village round a triangular green, with a manor house and a tiny 12th century Church near the present 19th century one.

PARK in the village called The Lee (900 043) 3km (2mi) N of Great Missenden.

1 Go NW along road passing R of church. 2 When road turns R go on along track. 3 At junction of several tracks go L over stile by iron gate. On by low grass bank. Halfway across field turn R to stile. 4 Here go ⅓ R and follow fence (on yr L) to wood.. 5 On along track in trees. Turn R at corner of wood. Keep along outside of wood. 6 On over road and down field (hedge on yr R). 7 At pines, on down fields past end of small wood and on to road (now a hedge on yr R). 8 L along road. 9 R up shady track. 10 On up path where track narrows. 11 At top L along path. 12 Turn L along path 20m after reaching wood. 13 On emerging carry on along edge of field. 14 Later it bears R then L. About 50m further on, go R down through small gap in large hedge. On down field, over stile and across next field to bridge. ● 15 Here R, aiming just R of line of houses. 16 At road L, then soon R up field edge (hedge on yr L). 17 On reaching a road bear L along it. 18 Over main road & ½ R along path. Soon on along larger path. 19 Near wood edge go sharp L down valley track. 20 Just before wood ends, go R up path near its edge. 21 At top wood corner go L along grass track & soon L again down track. Later go under railway. 22 Just before main road, turn R over grass (hedge on yr L). 23 After passing school, and just after passing by 3 trees, turn L over road and on along track to field. 24 ½ L up field to bridge and over it. 25 On past church up R fork of the two drives. Where drive levels go on up path to road. 26 On over road and up Frith Hill for 80m. Then fork L along track. 27 When track bears R to house, go on through small iron gate, now with fence on yr R. 28 Through iron gate and on in wood. 29 When wood ends go L down field (hedge on yr L) to road. 30 Over road and on down road 30m to stile. 31 Here R over field to stile at far corner. 32 On 20m to next stile & R over road. Then ½ L up field over stile, stile in hedge and third stile. 33 Now bear ½ R keeping near hedge on yr R. Then on up field to stile. 34 On over stile towards cables, soon by hedge on yr R. On over second stile, to far end of field. 35 Over stile at this field's L corner, then R along hedge past water tower to road. 36 R along road 100m then sharp L (120°) over field to stile in hedge. Here over 2 near stiles and on to field corner. 37 Here on to stile by pole at field corner. 38 On over field to gate in far corner. 39 On along shady track (later roughly surfaced). 40 Cross road and on along small road in The Lee. (To reach 2 go L on reaching larger road).

27A NORTH OF GREAT MISSENDEN (9km, 5¾ mi, 4.1cpm)

Follow 1 to 14 then ½ L under railway and on to road. A R along road 50m then L into field. At once turn R to gate in hedge. B On over next field to its far L corner. 32 Here cross road & go ½ L up field over stile, stile in hedge & 3rd stile. Now follow 33 to 40.

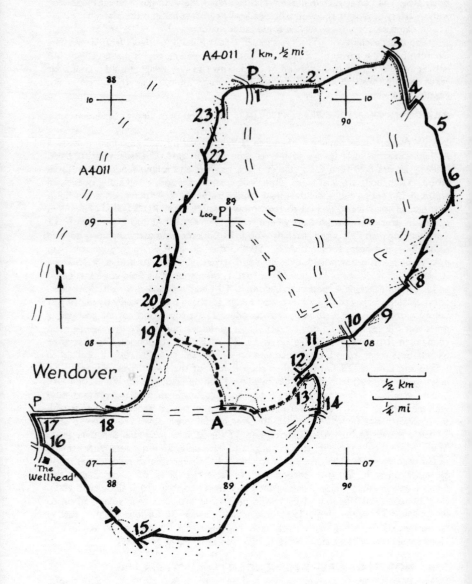

A4011 1 km, ½ mi

A4011

Wendover

'The Wellhead'

½ km
¼ mi

N

28 WENDOVER WOODS (13km, 8mi, 4.7cpm)

The walk introduces you to the attractive Wendover Woods, with the enclosed sections relieved by a number of open stretches and views. The walk skirts Wendover, passing not far from the large 14th century Church with an interesting brass memorial (1539). There are some 16th century houses and thatched cottages in the town.

From 14 there can be a long muddy section, best avoided by turning back and following the shorter walk. Sometimes mud at 4 and 6.

PARKING. Turn S off the A4011 3.5km (2¼ mi) NE from Wendover & park at top of hill (891 102).

1 Go E along track on same side of road as car park. 2 Go ⅓ L along path at gate by house. 3 R along road. 4 At road junction, go L 100m and R along shady path. 5 On along lane. 6 When lane turns L, you go R into Pavis Wood along its bottom edge. 7 When path comes in from R, go L along path which soon turns R and climbs in wood. 8 At road, L 50m, R over stile and across field. Look for large gap with pines each end. Aim for stile at the L side of gap. 9 Here, on by wood on yr L. 10 On over road. 11 Just before sunken track descends, climb the R bank. Go on down bank in wood. Later path gently bears away from track below. 12 At bottom of small dip, ignore paths going on up and R up. Instead, turn L down to track. • 13 Here, L up track, soon on parallel path close by fence (on yr R). Soon R along path (at first along wood edge). 14 At road, go R 20m and L along track. Much later it narrows near gate and stile. Keep on, following acorn signs along path, at first level, later gently descending. 15 Soon after joining track, go R at T-junction. Pass farm. 16 R along road. 17 R along road. 18 ½ L up track at forest sign. 19 Later wide track comes in on R. Bear L up this to gate at top. 20 Here, R along gravel track and at once ½ L along grass track. 21 Go on up at fork. 22 ½ R up steps. Later go on over drive. 23 After path levels look for path taking you 50m up to gate on yr R. Through gate & along track.

28A SHORTER WALK (9km, 5½ mi. 5.1cpm)

Follow 1-12, then R down track and on along road. A R up track along wood edge. Later track runs inside wood slightly away from edge. Ignore side tracks. Through gate at top. Follow 20 to 23.

29 FROM TRING (11½ km, 7¼ mi, 4cpm)

After passing through the attractive Tring Park there follows a lengthy flat open section (6-11) and a further flat passage through woods before reaching an enjoyable view (13-15). After a wood there is an open section, mainly on small roads, with good views. Finally a shady climb and the descent of an open ridge back to Tring. The Natural History Museum specialises in birds, butterflies, moths and mammals. The Church (15th century) is impressive and contains interesting monuments, rood-screen etc.

Muddy patches in some of the woods can usually be by-passed and the gentle gradients and stretches of road make this an easy walk.

PARK near museum (924 111) in Tring, S off the A4251.

1 At end of road to museum, go E to end of small road and R along enclosed path. **2** Over bridge and on parallel to road for 70m. Then ½ R beside fence (on yr L). **3** At wood, go L over stile and along track 10m. Then ½ R up clear path. On over another path and track. **4** At signpost, go on to gate near lodge. **5** Through gate and at once R over stile (gardens on yr L). **6** R with path when it turns to follow fence. **7** Soon over stile and L along field edge (gardens on yr L). **8** Over stile and R along track. **9** At roads, keep on (signed Hastoe). **10** On at

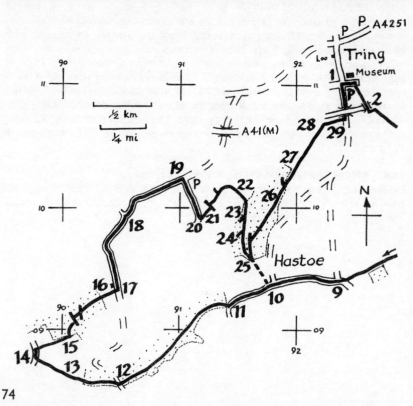

74

T-junction. **11** Where road turns L, enter wood and keep on along its edge (on yr L). **12** Over road & ¹/₂ R along path by wood edge. **13** On over field (hedge on yr L) and through 2 gates. **14** R along road 70m, then R over stile and across field to stile at wood corner. On beside wood edge to stile 80m before field corner. **15** L over stile along path in wood. L at grassy track for 50m. R down path between pines. On over grassy track (careful — animal holes on path). **16** On over field (fence on yr R) and on at its corner. **17** L along lane. **18** On at T-junction. **19** R at next T-junction. **20** Where road turns R, go L up field. **21** Over stile in hedge, L 5m and then R. Ignore track coming in on L. **22** Into wood and R along edge. **23** When larger track rises, take it and ignore path that forks R along edge. **24** L (and up) at next fork. Ignore smaller side paths. On and up until path passes to R of house. ● **25** After house, go sharp L down stony track 100m, then ¹/₂ R along path at signpost. On when path crosses yours. **26** Later path runs along wood edge. At track going ¹/₂ L down, leave wood and go on outside wood. **27** On when wood ends. At hedges, go on with hedge on yr R. **28** At field corner, go ¹/₂ R along fence (parallel to new road). **29** At small road go L, then R.

29A   SHORTER WALK (6¹/₂ km, 4¹/₄ mi, 4cpm)
PARKING. At W end of Tring, leave the A4251 and go SW along minor road ³/₄ km (¹/₂ mi) to T-junction (911 102).

Walk SE along lane. Follow 20 to 24. Then keep on to road & R along it. Now follow 11 to 18.

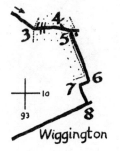

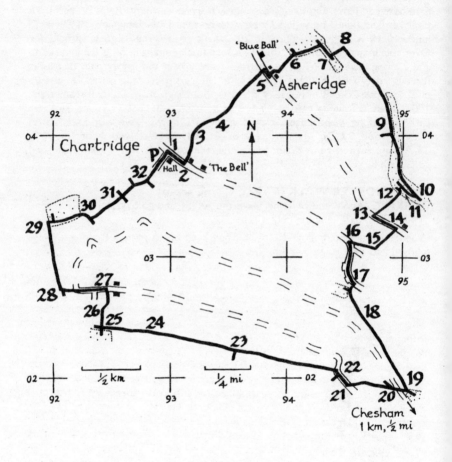

'Blue Ball'

Asheridge

Chartridge

P

Hall   'The Bell'

N

Chesham
1 km, ½ mi

½ km   ¼ mi

30 CHESHAM RIDGES (11½ km, 7¼ mi, 4.4cpm)

First Chartridge is descended and Asheridge crossed. Then there is an excellent path (8-11) high up on the next ridge, with attractive views, before entering a fine strip of beechwood. Further ups and downs bring you to a valley track (Herbert's Hole 22-25) and a scenic crossing of yet another ridge before the final climb. A 100m detour at 27 brings you to Pednor House Farm, where the lane goes through the courtyard of this 15th century house with attractive barns and dovecot.

The valley track may be muddy in places.

PARK in Cogdells Lane (929 038) a side turning in Chartridge 300m NW of 'The Bell'.

1 Go R (SE) 170m along main road. 2 Turn L just before chapel. At field go on down its edge, soon between hedges. 3 Out into field & on along its edge (hedge on yr R). 4 When hedge turns R, keep on down & up field towards L of several houses seen through wide gap in trees. Near top go on by hedge on yr L. 5 Turn R along road, then L into farm. Soon ½ R for 20m then ½ L. 6 On down track in wood and R along it at bottom. 7 Watch for gap on L. Go L here and up to top of field. 8 Here go R. For some time path follows top edge of fields. 9 When fence on yr R turns R at path junction, go into wood gently up to its top edge. Ignore minor paths off it. After path bears away from top edge, watch for pit on yr L. 10 Here sharp R along small path running parallel to lower wood edge. 11 After passing holly bushes turn L at path junction, soon bearing L to wood edge. 12 Leave wood down path between fence and hedge. 13 L along road. 14 Just before farm, go R over stile up field. 15 At top (20m from wire fence running up field), go under metal rail and between fences to road. 16 L along road and R at fork. 17 R down track at end of 2nd layby. Soon on down where track goes R. Path soon bears L. 18 Carry on along top edge of field to gate and on to stile. 19 Here sharp R down to wooden gate at road. 20 Over road into field. Take the L of 2 paths, aiming towards valley. Over stile into next field. Bear slightly L to stile at road. 21 R along road. 22 Turn L at second track. It runs along valley bottom. 23 When track turns L, go on with fence on yr R. Later through gate (hedge on yr L). Make for small gate ahead. 24 On through this gate to end of field, then through small gate to path between fences. 25 At cross path (200m before cottage) go R up hill to stile. 26 Over stile and ½ R to stile. Over it and along path to road. 27 L at road. On along track when road goes R. 28 On over stile (where track goes L) for 10m, then R over stile and along field edges (hedge on yr R). 29 After short descent, turn R over stile into wood. 30 On out of wood by fence on yr R, to field corner, then L down field (hedge on yr R). 31 At bottom, go on up (hedge on yr R) to stile at top R field corner. 32 Keep on between hedges to road.

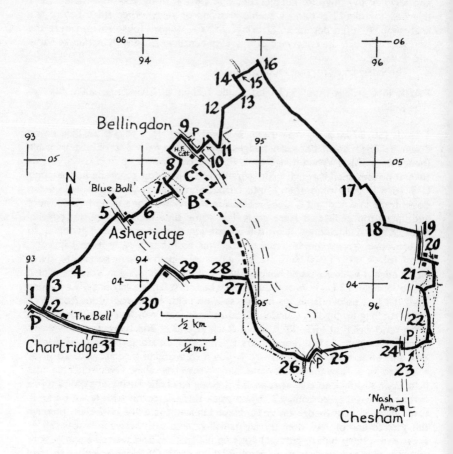

06 94

06 96

16

14 15

12 13

Bellingdon 9 P

93 05

H.F. Cott.

8 C

95 05

'Blue Ball' 7

10 11

N

B 17

5 6

Asheridge

18 19

93 94 A 20

04 04 96 21

4 29 28

3 30 27 95

1 .2

P 'The Bell' ½ km 26 P 25 24

Chartridge 31 ¼ mi 23

'Nash Arms'

Chesham

78

31 MORE CHESHAM RIDGES (11½ km, 7mi, 5.3cpm)

This walk is similar in character to the previous one and is included to introduce you to the exceptionally long, open and scenic Hawridge (16-17), as well as to some other good paths over the other ridges. There are views nearly all the way and three small attractive beech woods.

PARK in Cogdells Lane (929 038) a side turning in Chartridge 300m NW of 'The Bell'.

1 Go R (SE) 170m along main road. 2 Turn L just before chapel. At field go on down its edge, soon between hedges. 3 Out into field & on along its edge (hedge on yr R). 4 When hedge turns R, keep on down & up field towards L of several houses seen through wide gap in trees. Near top go on by hedge on yr L. 5 Turn R along road, then L into farm. Soon ½ R for 20m then ½ L. 6 On down track in wood and L at bottom. 7 Look for metal farm gate up to yr R and then aim for stile 50m to its L. Over stile and up field (hedge on yr L). 8 At top corner turn L for 150m. Here R over stile and on. 9 R at road and L along 2nd drive on yr L (opposite Huge Farm Cott.) 10 On along path into thicket. Soon go R into field. On along its edge to corner. 11 Here go sharp L, to pass jutting out field corner and reach metal farm gate in far corner. 12 Through gate and ½ R down to double stile at valley bottom. 13 Over both and L for 100m to field corner. 14 Over stile and R (hedge on yr R) to end of line of trees. 15 R through gate and at once L up to stile. Over and on to ridge top (hedge on yr R). 16 Here R through gap and along ridge, at first with hedge on yr L. 17 When ridge path ends, turn L 100m along hedge (on yr L) and R along hedge (on yr L). 18 On reaching corner turn L along track (under cables). 19 R at road and L at farm. Up by buildings until house is seen just L. 20 Go R along the hedge that starts opposite house. 21 On inside wood 60m until hedge is seen to L dividing 2 fields. Opposite this go R down towards buildings (path soon clear). At wider path bear L up it. 22 By a pit on yr L (100m before end of wood) take R fork. At fence ½ R to follow it down to wood corner. 23 Over stile and down (hedge on yr L) to road. 24 Here, R and soon L along path (houses on yr L) parallel to cables. 25 R along road 50m, then L along road 100m. 26 Here go into wood. Soon bear R to keep on path about 20m below top edge of wood. (Ignore minor paths). Later you reach top edge and then go gently down to bottom edge. ● 27 Here turn L along hedge down to valley bottom and up 100m to stile. 28 Over stile and up, now with hedge on yr R. 29 At road go R then L at Tiles Farm. Soon through farm gate and on by hedge on yr R to small gate at valley bottom. 30 Here on between hedges and on along drive. 31 R along road.

31A SHORTER WALK (8km, 5mi, 4.4cpm)
PARK in quiet side road at Bellingdon (994 051).

Go along drive opposite Huge Farm Cottage. Follow 10-26, then on along bottom edge of wood. A On along top edge of fields to corner stile by big holly tree. B Here go R, then L over stile 100m before house. Along field edge to poles. C Here over stile and R to road. Then L along road to start. (To continue walk go R along drive after 50m).

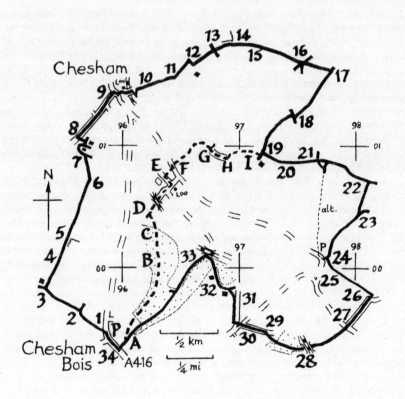

Chesham

Chesham
Bois

N

½ km

¼ mi

A416

32 NEAR CHESHAM (11km, 7mi, 5.3cpm)

The walk passes through some charming old parts of Chesham. (There are some 17th century buildings in the High Street, and St. Mary's Church — with a 12th century window — is worth a visit). Outside the town there is a remarkable amount of unspoilt open hilly country with rapidly changing views. There are also the attractive woods, a beautiful 13th century Church at Chesham Bois, and the River Chess — not much more than a stream, but even this is unusual in a Chiltern walk.

There may be one or two muddy patches. The worst section (21-22) can be by-passed by going S along the valley track and L along the road to 24.

PARK in quiet side road at Chesham Bois (958 994) near bend in the A416, 2km (1¼ mi) S of Chesham.

1 At bend in road go (NW) along Mayhall Lane. 2 Fork L at lane end. 3 Just before farm turn R. Soon over 2 stiles and on with hedge on yr L. 4 On into next fields. Hedge now on yr R. 5 On down fields when hedge goes R. 6 Through gate at flat bottom of field and ½ L to houses. 7 L along winding road, then L twice to reach larger road. 8 R down road to Chesham. 9 Cross main road and go R 20m. Make for the steps (100m away up side road). On over railway and R 50m, sharp L 50m, and R up hill. 10 At open field, go on up to corner stile. 11 Over stile and ½ L along hedge (on yr L). R at corner. 12 L at blue gate across field to stile. 13 On over farm track, now by hedge (on yr L). 14 When hedge turns L, go on over field. Aim just R of distant tall mast, to reach stile in hedge. 15 Over stile and down to bottom. 16 On up field edge (fence on yr L). 17 Go R on reaching crossing fence and down to bottom (fence on yr L). 18 Go R 20m and L up track. ● 19 70m before farm go L over stile and field to 2nd stile. 20 On down fields (hedge on yr L). 21 On over track and 50m of field. On up shady track. 22 Look for gap at top of rise. Here go R between fence and hedge. 23 On down shady track. 24 Just before road, go L through gate and along bank to stile. 25 On in next field. 26 R along drive 20m to road. On to main road. 27 Over road, through gate and soon over stile. On by fence on yr R to pass under railway. 28 On into wood. Keep to main track. It later narrows. 29 On along road 200m. 30 At T-junction, go on along footpath. Cross road it reaches, climb bank and turn R along path. 31 ½ L over stile and field. Over 2nd stile and L along stony lane. Bear R after passing Church. 32 At footpath sign go on (passing by Warren Cottage on yr L) and down path. Down steps and ½ L for 50m. 33 L along track. 34 R along main road.

32A SHORTER WALK (8km, 5mi, 6.2cpm)

From bend in main road, go SE 150m along it and L down track for 100m. **A** Here fork L along path. **B** When fence on yr L ends go on down main path to wood edge. **C** ½ L down field. **D** ½ R down track. On under railway and along road. Turn L just after passing tennis courts. **E** R at end of row of houses, over river to main road. **F** Here L 20m, then R up Trapps Lane. It narrows later to a surfaced path. **G** When path ends, go on along Larks Rise to gate. **H** L along field edge (hedge on yr L) to corner stile. **I** Here, L along track 20m, then R over stile and field to 2nd stile. Now follow 20-33.

32B SHORTER WALK (8½ km, 5¼ mi, 4.8cpm)

Follow 1-18, then just before farm turn R along field edge (hedge on yr R) and down to kissing gate. **H** Through gate and along road. **G** At sign 'Pheasant Ride,' go on along surfaced path (houses on yr L). At sign 'Whichcote Gardens', go ½ L down wider track to main road. **F** On over road and bridge. **E** L along road, then R at T-junction. Over stream. On up Hodds Wood Road and on under railway. **D** 100m further on at stile, go ½ L up field to wood. **C** Here, on up wood. **B** At top, fence appears on yr R. Keep by it until larger track is met. **A** On to road and R.

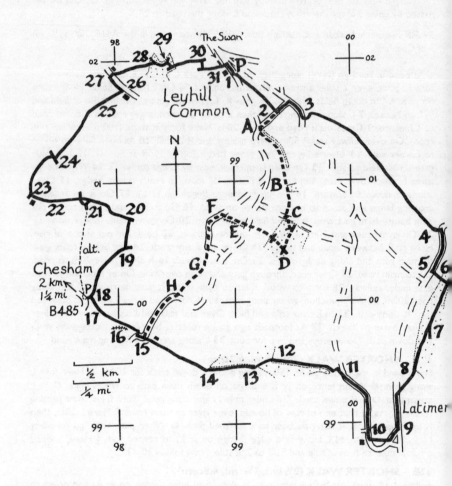

'The Swan'

98
02   29
28
27   26
25

30
31 P
1
2
3

Leyhill
Common

A

N

99

01

B

F   C

E

D

G

4

5

6

H

Chesham
2 km
1¼ mi
B485

P
18
17

00

16
15

12

14   13

11

17

8

½ km
¼ mi

00

Latimer

99

99

10

9

82

33 LEYHILL TO LATIMER (12km, 7½ mi, 4.7cpm)

After a flat start there is a good open ridge (3-6) and further views (10) near Latimer. After a glimpse or two of the River Chess, there is a hilly return with a good selection of views except where these are obscured by the shrubs that line both sides of some of the old lanes.

There may be some muddy patches, especially at 22-23. Save it for a dry season, or at 20, go on along road 100m, then R through gate and up track to small gate. On between hedges to join walk at 23.

PARK by the inn at Leyhill Common (990 019).

1 Go SE over golf course between 2 roads. • 2 L along road, R at T-junction. 3 When road bends ½ R, turn L on track which bears L, then R, and then goes straight along a broad ridge. 4 R along road. 5 L up into wood at signpost. 6 At top of wood, turn R along track inside wood. 7 At fork, go down R. 8 On leaving wood, go through gate and down track to road and L along it. 9 At green triangle, turn ½ R. After 50m, go R up path between railings. On over field, through gate to road. 10 R along road. 11 Where road bends R, go on over stile & field, then L 30m & R along wood edge. 12 At far field corner, go down into wood. 13 On leaving wood, go ½ R along field edge. 14 Through gate and along field edge with hedge on yr L. On in next fields, and past barn on yr R. 15 On along road 50m, then R along drive for 20m and L. On through gate first by wall, then fence. 16 As fence bears L keep on along path. 17 Over stile at end of field. On along bank to gate. 18 R up enclosed track (soon ignore gate into field on R). 19 At fork keep on along field edge between hedge and fence. 20 L along track. 21 At bottom, where track bends L, go on 50m over field, cross track and on up field edges (hedge on yr R). 22 On reaching open field, go on to stile 70m R of farm. 23 Here, R along track. 24 At bottom, R for 20m, then L up by fence (on yr R). At top field corner, ½ R along next field edge. 25 At field corner, go over stile and on to stile just L of pub. 26 Don't climb stile, but go L 150m down field edge to stile. 27 Here, cross road and go just into drive. Then over stile on the R and diagonally over field to double stile. On over next field to stile in far corner. 28 Here, on in wood bearing L to keep near wood edge on yr L. 29 Just after path gets to wood edge, turn R along path. Then L along larger path, soon reaching wood edge. Here, on to open field and on over field (hedge on yr L). On over corner stile and between fences. 30 R along road to end and L along rough road. 31 R along road.

33A SOUTH FROM LEYHILL (8km, 5mi, 5.7cpm)

Follow 1, then R along road. **A** L at bottom along field edge (wood on yr L, then fence). **B** At field corner, go over 2 stiles & on through small wood, then over field (hedge on yr R). **C** Go L along road 20m, then ½ R along path in wood. At track go L 20m, then sharp R along track. **D** Turn R along crossing track. On over field. **E** Over road and on by fence. **F** L along road, passing White End Park. On over field when road goes L. **G** Over stile in hedge and ⅓ R down to corner stile. **H** On down road. After it bends R, go R along drive (Blackwell Lodge) for 20m and L. On through gate first by wall, then fence. Now follow 16-31.

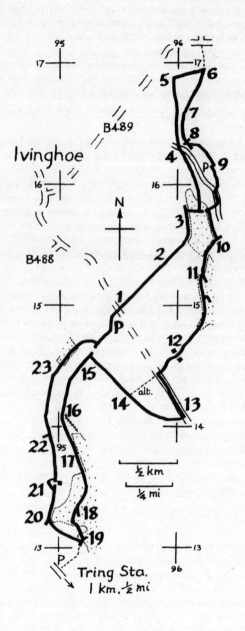

95
17

96
17

5   6

7

8

4   P 9

B489

Ivinghoe

16

16

N

3

2   10

11

1

15

P

12

23

15

14   alt.   13

16   14

22
95   17

21

18

20   19

13   13

P   96

½ km
¼ mi

Tring Sta.
1 km. ½ mi

B488

34 IVINGHOE HILLS (11km, 7mi, 4cpm)

A beautiful walk, never far from the ridge and so with plenty of views. Pitstone Mill, one of England's oldest post windmills (one beam is marked 1627) can be seen in the distance (so unfortunately can the cement works. Birmingham can also be seen, or so some say). The Beacon has traces of an Iron Age fort (600B.C.). Aldbury Nowers is an attractive beech-covered hill near the old village of Aldbury.

The path from 13-14 does not seem to exist, so you can't tell if you are on it. Therefore you might regard a direct route along a farm track from 12-14 as less of a trespass.

PARK in the car park (954 149) 1 km (½ mi) SE along minor road leaving the B488 at a bend just S of Ivinghoe.

1 From car park cross road and on (NE) over field. 2 On over stile. Path soon bends L. •3 On over stile 100m, then sharpish R along track and later L along path into open. On towards Beacon down grass track (later in trees). 4 On over road along gently rising path just R of nearest hillock. 5 At the Beacon (reached after slight dip), turn R. 6 At fence, go sharp R. 7 Path bears L, keeping near shrubs (on yr L). 8 Over track and on for 40m (road 30m to yr R). ²/₃ L over stile for 100m (fence on yr L), then ½ R down and up to stile. 9 On along car park track. On along road 50m, then ½ R along track. Soon bear L to walk by line of posts. 10 R along track. 11 Fork ½ R down track when your track is seen bending R ahead. Soon on down when larger track is met. 12 On through farm. L along road. 13 R over stile and along by hedge (on yr L). There is no path. Where hedge bends L, go on over field towards long straight fence leading to slight dip in ridge (if there are crops it may be better to go round field edge). 14 On over farm track, with fence on yr L. • 15 Over stile and L along by fence. 16 Where fence bends L, gently leave it (¹/₃ L) down vague path to stile. (If you stay by fence, go R down outside wood 70m to stile). 17 Over stile and along path. Later path enters wood. 18 Fork R (after slight descent) soon reaching wood edge. Then bear L inside wood and ½ R along path over open ground into wood again. 19 R at track for 10m, then ½ R along small path. 20 ½ R along drive. 21 At house, ½ L between hedges. Soon L along track with hedge or fence on yr L. Over 2 stiles. 22 On over the R hand of 2 stiles 10m apart. Follow vague paths bearing R round bottom of hill. The quarry fence is a guide. 23 Near end of quarry, path climbs on in trees, soon on the crest of a 'mini-ridge'. On leaving wood this bears R, soon reaching fence. Here go L along path to car park.

34A TO ALDBURY NOWERS (7½ km, 4½ mi, 4cpm)
Follow 1-2, then on over stile 100m and sharpish R along track. In the open, turn R to walk by line of posts. Now follow 10-23.

34B TO IVINGHOE BEACON (8½ km, 5¼ mi, 4cpm)
Follow 1-14, then over stile and R to start.

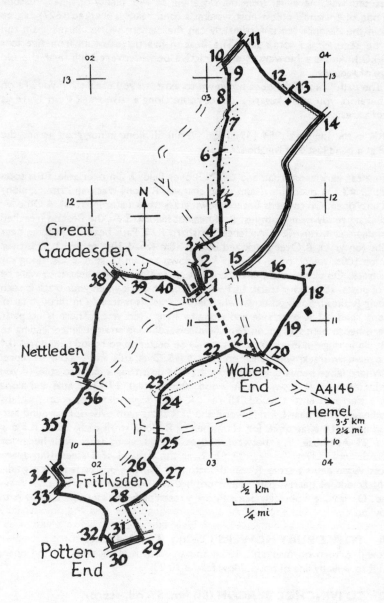

11
10
9
12
13
8
14
7
6
5
4
3
2
Great
Gaddesden
P
15
16
17
38
18
39 40
Inn
19
Nettleden
21 20
37
22
Water
End
36
23
35
24
A4146
Hemel
34
25
3.5 km
2¼ mi
Frithsden
26
27
33
28
32 31
29
Potten
30
End

N

½ km
¼ mi

13
02
04
13
03
12
12
11
11
10
02
03
04
10

35 AROUND GREAT GADDESDEN (12½ km, 7¾ mi, 5.3cpm)

After crossing the River Gade there are good views before entering Hoo Wood. Then there is a flattish section before more views near Gaddesden Place. The second half has a greater variety of views as you go over the ridges from Frithsden to Nettleden and then over to Great Gaddesden, where the 14th century Church contains Romans bricks and tiles in its walls.
It can be muddy from 32 to 33.

PARK at Great Gaddesden near the church (029 113), reached by turning off the A4146 at a crossroad N of Hemel Hempstead & soon turning R along side road.

1 Go on (NW) along side road. 2 50m before swings, go R over stile, ½ L across field and over 2nd stile. 3 Bear R to bridge and on to stile in hedge. 4 Over road, up concrete drive and on along field edge. Soon bear L with hedge. When hedge bends R, keep on up into wood. 5 Ignore R fork just inside wood and another R fork later on. 6 On over crossing track. 7 10m before wooden fence bars progress, go L along path, which soon reaches gate. Down field edge (hedge on yr R). 8 At bottom, go through gate and on by same hedge, now on yr L. 9 Over gate in field corner and on (hedge now on R). 10 R along road. 11 R at signpost opposite farm. On by 2 field edges (hedge on yr L). 12 Over stile in corner of 2nd field. On 100m, & L to stile. 13 Over stile & R along hedge (on yr R). 14 R at road. 15 At road junction, sharp L over fence and up along bottom of shallow valley. 16 On through fence gap, now with fence on yr L. 17 Turn R along next fence met. At iron gate go ½ R to stile & on. 18 On down field. Aim between 2 groups of houses below. 19 Soon over 2 stiles. Aim to pass close to L house of R group. 20 Out to road, R 10m, then L between buildings, over stile and bridge, and on to field corner. ● 21 Here, ½ L over stile and along by hedge (on yr R). 22 At wood, on along path near R edge. 23 After passing through some pines, path bears L, & soon reaches stile at wood edge. 24 On to road and over. 25 On 200m along path. 26 Turn L with path to hedge corner. 27 At hedge corner turn R, keeping hedge on yr L. On in next field, keeping close to fence. 28 Go L into wood at stile and on by wire fence (on yr L). 29 R at road. 30 R down Browns Spring (at shops). 31 On when road goes R. 32 Soon turn R along track. 33 R at road, then fork L. 34 R just after passing Alford Arms and up steep track. 35 At top, go L over R hand of 2 stiles and R along field edge, later between wire fences. 36 On down track and L 20m at road. 37 Here, R by hedge (on yr R) up to road. 38 Here, L 50m, over stile on yr R and along wood edge. 39 At end of wood, go over stile and on over field. On to double poles by hedge. 40 Here, over stile. Across field to L end of wall under trees. Go along by wall and L over stile. (To carry on, go sharp L at phone box and follow 2 onwards).

35A NORTH FROM GREAT GADDESDEN (7km, 4¼ mi, 4.9cpm)
Follow 1-20, then ½ R along hedge (on yr R).

35B SOUTH FROM GREAT GADDESDEN (6½ km, 4mi, 5cpm)
Go SE along path opposite the Cock & Bottle. At 2 stiles in field corner, go over stile, R over 2nd stile and on by hedge (on yr R). Then follow 22-40.

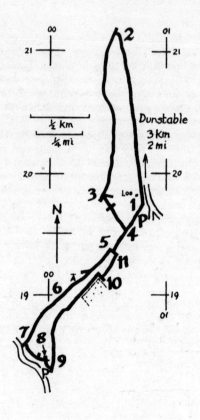

2

21 —|— 00   01 —|— 21

½ km

¼ mi

Dunstable
3 km
2 mi

20 —|—   —|— 20

3   Loo   1
     4 P

N

5   4

11

6   00   10

19 —|—   —|— 19
     01

7   8

9

36   DUNSTABLE DOWNS (6½ km, 4¼ mi, 4cpm)

A short but fine open walk, mostly on or near the top of the downs, with good views. At the southern end of the walk you can see the Whipsnade (chalk) Lion and other foreign animals. To the north, many specimens of Homo Sapiens will be seen at the weekends, also gliders floating effortlessly on the breeze. The 'Five Knolls' at the northern tip of the walk are burial mounds from Neolithic and Bronze Ages.

PARKING. Start leaving Dunstable along the B489. At the outskirts turn L along a B road to park at the top of the downs (008 197).

1 Go N (towards Dunstable) along top of down. 2 When you descend, go on to smooth green field, and there go L 20m, and L again along shady path. Later, always follow path near bottom of downs (where there are cultivated fields). 3 Watch for a small dip beside an 8m length of wood fencing (on yr R). Here turn ½ L up small path soon with dense shrubs on yr R. Keep on up over track. 4 Turn R along bottom edge of field. Keep straight on over 100m wide strip of grass on yr R. 5 Just before gate go R 50m, & L along field edge passing by 2 pylons. (Ignore path going ½ R before pylons are reached). 6 On down R bank of sunken track. 7 Over stile 15m before road & L up path. Go on past 4-way sign post. 8 ½ R along path to car park. On up steps & L for 100m along field edge to gate. 9 Through gate & on along level path by field edge (hedge on yr R). 10 At far corner of wood (on yr R) go R & soon L to far corner of field. 11 Here go L 80m to gate (already seen at point 5) & R back to start.

Little Missenden Church (Walk 21)

The Chiltern Gentian

Roadside Poppies

Wild Rose

POSTSCRIPT

I hope you have enjoyed these walks. If you come across any difficulties I would like to hear from you c/o the Publisher. I won't promise to reply individually, but will look into them for the next update.

CHECK LIST

Weather Forecast

Rucksack (first aid for minor problems; food (plastic box is a useful holder); drink; boxes for collecting blackberries etc.)

Walking shoes

Suitable clothes for wet or cold weather

Sunglasses

Details of proposed walk e.g. this book

Maps (a) road map for travelling to start of walk
       (b) 1:50000 map of the walk

Compass

Pencil and paper

Key to get back indoors

Money for fares, petrol etc.

Membership cards/permits etc., for nature reserves, National Trust etc.

Optional: camera and accessories, binoculars, books for identification of whatever you feel like identifying.

Looking towards Radnage (Walk 15, stage 14)

Swyncombe Downs (Walk 1)

Above Fawley Court Farm (Walk 9)

Looking down from the ridge (Walk 30, stage 8)

Looking South along Dunstable Downs (Walk 36)

Final descent to Cockshoots Wood (Walk 26)

INDEX (Bold figures: walk number. Other figures: page number)